Short Flights

Thirty-Two Modern Writers Share Aphorisms of Insight, Inspiration, and Wit

EDITED BY

James Lough and Alex Stein

schaffner
press

SCHAFFNER PRESS
TUCSON, ARIZONA

Aphorisms or essays by the following authors first appeared in these venues:

John Bradley: *Hotel Amerika*; *Trancelumination* (Lowbrow Press).

Alfred Corn: *The Pith Helmet* (Cummington Press); and *Salamagundi*.

Sharon Dolin: *Denver Quarterly*, and the *Kenyon Review Online*; essay first appeared in *The American Poet*.

Thomas Farber: *The End of My Wits* (El Leon Literary Arts).

Kevin Griffith: *Hotel Amerika*.

H. L. Hix: *Spirits Hovering Over the Ashes: Legacies of Postmodern Theory* (SUNY Press); *First Fire, Then Birds* (Etruscan Press).

Yahia Lababidi: *Signposts to Elsewhere* (Jane Street Press)

Ann Lauinger: *Hotel Amerika; Against Butterflies* (Little Red Tree Publishing)*; Persuasions of Fall* (University of Utah Press).

Dan Liebert: *The Yale Review*; *Barrow Street*; *The London Magazine*; *Exquisite Corpse*; *New Orleans Review*; *Michigan Quarterly Review*; *Hotel Amerika*; *Mayday*; *Cold Mountain Review*; *FragLit*; *All Aphorisms All the Time*.

James Lough: *Hotel Amerika*.

James Richardson: *Vectors* (Copper Canyon Press, previously Ausable Press).

Charles Simic: *The Monster Loves his Labyrinth* (Copper Canyon Press, previously Ausable Press).

David Shields: *Reality Hunger* (Knopf).

Michael Theune: *The Iowa Review*, *Seven Corners* blog.

Contents

Preface by Alex Stein • ix

Introduction, "Varieties of Aphoristic Experience:
A Breviary of the Briefest Genre," by James Lough • xi

Aphorisms

James Richardson • 1

Charles Simic • 11

James Lough • 18

Sara Levine • 28

Sharon Dolin • 31

H.L. Hix • 39

Ashleigh Brilliant • 47

Yahia Lababidi • 54

Brian Jay Stanley • 61

Dan Liebert • 67

David Shields • 73

Richard Kostelanetz • 78

Ann Lauinger • 84

Holly Woodward • 89

Steven Carter • 94

George Murray • 101

Alex Stein • 112

Hart Pomerantz • 120

James Guida • 126

Lily Akerman • 132

Charles Bernstein • 139

Olivia Dresher • 149

Irena Karafilly • 154

Christopher Cokinos • 159

Michael Theune • 163

Stephen Dobyns • 168

Alfred Corn • 176

Eric Nelson • 187

James Geary • 193

Thomas Farber • 199

Kevin Griffith • 203

John Bradley • 211

Afterword
"When Very Little is Required in the Classroom:
On Teaching the Long-Winded Writer to Write Short,"
by Sara Levine • 216

Author Bios • 224

Short Flights

Preface

by

ALEX STEIN

James Lough and I conceived this project several years
ago after attending a panel discussion at a convention
in Chicago. Panelist Sara Levine spoke about teaching
the aphorism and was flawlessly entertaining. James
Richardson's little aphorisms were getting big laughs from
the audience.

During the question and answer portion I asked the
panel why there were no anthologies of contemporary
aphorists. There was a general, abashed consensus among
the panelists that the audience did not exist for such an
undertaking. "But surely," I called out, "the same can be
said for anthologies of contemporary poets, and those are
getting published by the boatload."

The remaining audience seemed to get a kick out
of the phrase, "by the boatload," in this context, but talk
shifted elsewhere.

When the panel concluded I gathered contact
information from Richardson and Levine. Richardson could
get me in touch with James Geary, whose best-selling
book, "The World in a Phrase," was being called "the

definitive work" on the subject of aphorism and whose literary blog "All Aphorisms, All the Time," convened many of the best contemporary aphorists into one convenient forum.

"I think we should do this," I said to Lough, who was waiting by the exit, talking to his wife on the phone.

"What?" he asked, covering the mouthpiece.

"I think we should put together an anthology of contemporary aphorists. It would be the first. I think we should do it."

"Oh, we are doing it, all right," James replied. "A gift like this doesn't get dropped in your lap every day."

Thanks for seeing it, James Lough. And for seeing it through. And many thanks to the writers whose aphorisms appear in these pages.

Varieties of Aphoristic Experience: A Breviary of the Briefest Genre

by

JAMES LOUGH

Time Stays, We Go

The aphorism is a very old kind of writing. It goes back at least as far as the Proverbs in the Hebrew bible and the Hindu sutras, which were spiritual instruction manuals from many centuries B.C.E.[1] Ancients had lots of spare time. Hunter-gatherers worked roughly twenty-hour weeks and early farmers had whole seasons off to contemplate the big questions: *What is the good life? Why are we here? How should I store my millet?* Hence, the aphorism was born.

But with all this time on their hands, why did they focus on cranking out mostly graffiti-length tidbits?

Because the ancients understood that much of their audience, rich in time, was poor in education. Most were barely literate, so the writers' pronouncements had better be brief and pack some punch. Life was short, the ancients understood, so grind wisdom down to its sharpest point.

---

1 In James Geary's book *The World in a Phrase: A Brief History of the Aphorism*, our foremost aphorism expert traces the aphorism's origin to the 5000-year-old Chinese oracular text, the *I Ching*.

The same policy works well for us today but for
different reasons. Moderns are much more educated, with
a world literacy rate of 84%. Our media of communication
have mushroomed almost infinitely. But our need for
bedrock insights is as urgent as ever. While most of us are
no longer preoccupied by tigers in the trees and enemies
over the hill, there is a shortage of what the ancients had
in spades: time. Our time is imperiled by tidal waves of
trivia, hectored by a hundred emails a day, collared by this
ad slogan or that list of things to do, each one sidetracking
our steady, focused awareness. As T.S. Eliot prophesied a
hundred years ago, we are "distracted from distraction by
distraction."

This unsteady stream of information can be
overwhelming. It can also have the effect of "flattening"
wisdom, knowledge and reflection into mere information.
As presented by our media, Aesop gets the same
15-second spot as Aflac and Dante's no richer than Dairy
Queen. Our internet experts have collapsed such cultural
achievements as deep thought, original insight and facility
with language into one distressingly broad generic term:
content. Stuff we pour between the pictures. The result?
We skim rather than absorb. Strapped for time, we spread
ourselves thin and grow shallow. We read Sappho or
Shakespeare the same way we glance over a tweet or a
text message, scanning for the gist, impatient to move on.
But you can't skim Shakespeare.

As a compromise with our busy era, we come back
to the aphorism, a quickly-digested little word morsel,
delightful and instructive, that condenses thought, insight,
and wordplay.[1] But don't let its convenience deceive
you – some aphorisms hit the tongue less like candy and

1 You'll notice some writers refer to their aphorisms as epigrams. Similarities do exist – for example, epigrams are short and
witty – the technical difference is that epigrams are little poems
that usually rhyme.

more like bitter pills. As James Geary puts it, "It must have a twist," or an element of surprise. A good aphorism will deceive us, drawing us north and instantly swerving south, beckoning us like a pretty little rug that yanks itself out from under our feet so we can examine it up close. A strong aphorism seduces, surprises, and sinks in.

Instruction and Insight

An aphorism can lead us in one of two basic philosophical directions. The first is the aphorism of *instruction*: the maxim or proverb. It tells you what to do and how to live.

Work as if you were to live 100 years, pray as if you were to die tomorrow.

—BENJAMIN FRANKLIN

The aphorism of instruction generally comes from a person who has ventured far in the world of affairs and wants to help us along a similar path. This kind of aphorism is homely and avuncular, practical like a stout walking stick. It upholds the status quo, preserves traditional values and worldviews. Its impulse is essentially *conservative*, to preserve and pass on what has worked in the past.

A bird in the hand is worth two in the bush.

The second philosophical approach is the aphorism of *insight*. The aphorism of insight is not a champion of tradition – it's an outlaw. It doesn't pretend to tell us what to do, though its goal is at least as presumptuous. It tells us how things *are*, tells us *what's what*, at a deeper level than common sense. Insight aphorisms penetrate. They see more deeply than most of us usually dare, or they come from startling vantage points:

It's cheaper to keep slaves eight hours a day, than twenty-four.

–JPJ[2]

This kind of aphorism cuts against the complacent common sense we've been fed since birth by parents, teachers, preachers, bosses, politicians and businessmen who may have meant well – or meant well for themselves. Insight aphorisms are *radical.* They uproot clichés and question authority:

Not strong morals, but weak stomachs, keep us from being vultures.

–JPJ

An insight aphorism is anarchic, a bomb exploding in an empty house, blasting out the windows, blowing the doors off their hinges, leaving the reader with a sense of catharsis, exhilaration and space.

Future, n. That period of time in which our affairs prosper, our friends are true and our happiness is assured.

—AMBROSE BIERCE

---

2 We know next to nothing about JPJ, the anonymous author of the excellent book *Last Aphorisms*. JPJ, if you happen to be reading this, give us a call.

Doubles, Anyone?

How can these little one-off sentences – so closely related to jokes, not to mention advertising slogans – profoundly influence how we see reality? How do the little word devices work? Geary provides a crucial clue with his prescription that an aphorism "must have a twist." This explains why a maxim like

Pride goeth before the fall

is useful knowledge but isn't a particularly engaging aphorism. There's no twist, nothing unexpected. It needs a reversal, or more generally, it needs to bear the double footprints of a thought retracing itself. A good aphorism's *doubleness* is what makes it pop. It undulates, airborne in two quick arcs – one up, one down – and snaps at the end with a wicked crack.

A man can be happy with any woman, so long as he does not love her.

—OSCAR WILDE

Nature loves doubles. Tree limbs, like blood vessels, divide and subdivide. Humans are forked beasts, our torsos branching into arms and legs, fingers and toes. More of us is two than one: eyes, ears, lungs, brain hemispheres, kidneys, testes, ovaries. Sure, the heart is a lonely pumper, but its motion is split into systole and diastole. Only the liver lives alone.

Likewise, our binary minds invent mythologies that abide in twos. God, dissatisfied with Oneness, split everything up, first into light and darkness, then into heaven and earth, and then, tiring of only one person, splintered Eve out of Adam for company. Since then, the myth goes, pairs are everywhere – in Janus, Libra, Gemini, yin and yang, Jekyll and Hyde. It takes two to tango, and if we're lucky, to head back home and make the beast with two backs.

Doubles dominate written language – black words on white pages – and especially in aphorisms, which carve language down to its crux. Irony and reversal, for example, are an aphorist's stock in trade: a line of syntax doubling into the unexpected.

I can resist anything except temptation.   –OSCAR WILDE

Or metaphor, where a word splits off into its analogical mirror:

It is the east, and Juliet is the sun.   — SHAKESPEARE

With paradox, it's a double truth staring into a carnival mirror:

This statement is false.

In a chiasmus, two phrases criss-cross to make a satisfying "X,"

It's not the men in your life that count – it's the life in your men.   –MAE WEST

And with a delicious pun, one mouth sound splits into double sense:

You can tune a guitar, but you can't tuna fish.

–DOUGLAS ADAMS

The aphorism's very doubleness enables it to follow Geary's dictum: *Do the twist.* It also supplies the element of surprise.

Size Matters

Writers love inventing new traditions, and in these pages you'll notice the broad variety of approaches they take to these slim fragments. At the most basic level, there's the issue of length. Most aphorisms are short, a sentence or two, but others are longer, whole paragraphs. According to Geary, the long-form aphorism, "a variant that borders on the parable but pulls up well short of the essay," has been around since at least the 15th century, with the likes of Balthasar Gracian in the 1500s and Arthur Schopenhauer in the 1800s. It's still alive and well. A long-form aphorism usually builds a short argument, step-by-step, climaxing with a final, punchy conclusion.

Human nature needs both fellowship and freedom, but usually we must choose. The more we encircle ourselves with others, the more we handcuff our will. Ask for help on a project at work, and it will not be done exactly how you want. Marry, and your holidays will be spent at in-laws'. Have children, and you will listen to their music in the car instead of yours. But worship your freedom, and you will be an empty temple. A bachelor's life resembles a widower's. Write, sing, or paint the way you please, disregarding the market's demands, and you will be your own and only audience. Travel wherever you want, whenever you want, and you will go alone. Fellowship imprisons us, freedom exiles us.

–BRIAN JAY STANLEY

Contrast this with short-form aphorists who skip the dialectical foreplay and climb straight to the climax, having already rehearsed the argument in their heads. But if Stanley had cut everything prior to his pessimistic conclusion:

Fellowship imprisons us, freedom exiles us.

All nuance would be gone. Without the gradual pumping up, the conclusion loses its air – even its meaning has changed. Music in the car, the bachelor and the widower – these give us emotional flavor and dimension that are hard to pull off in a one-liner. Long-form aphorisms are related to prose poems.

Whose Line is it, Anyway?

Another innovation in the aphorism has to do with *point of view*, or how much the aphorists allow themselves and other people to appear into their aphorisms. Traditionally, aphorisms have been told "from a distance," in the third-person objective, which gives them the quality, for better or worse, of a god-like authority.

God is a comedian playing to an audience too afraid to laugh.

–VOLTAIRE

Some writers, bowing to a more modest subjectivity, include themselves in the first-person:

I don't believe in God but I'm afraid of opening an umbrella in the house. 　　　　　　　–CHARLES SIMIC

Still others use the third-person personal, *he* and *she*, to write about other people in specific situations. I call these narrative aphorisms because they tell very short stories. Maybe we should call them situation aphorisms, like scenes in a sitcom:

A man sometimes seems annoyed when another man sits down beside him on the train. The thought seems to be "I was saving that for an unknown beautiful woman!"

　　　　　　　　　　　　　　　—JAMES GUIDA

I know that man is a mine of information; every time he speaks, I'm buried alive. 　　　　　　　–SARA LEVINE

And as for pure storytelling, there are of course actual stories, or parables, another kind of long-form aphorism that's been around since antiquity:

The Whispering Animals
On the day that animals acquired the power of speech, we were astounded to discover that they had nothing interesting to say! Nevertheless, we lay awake at night, restless, troubled, straining to hear them whispering about us.

　　　　　　　　　　　　　　　–STEVEN CARTER

The Gregueria

I'm pleased to end this introduction by presenting two additions to the aphoristic family. First, there's the fetching hybrid (or halforism?) called the *gregueria*. The gregueria was invented and named by the 20th Century Spanish writer Ramón Gómez de la Serna. He defined it as "humor plus metaphor," a poetic joke:

The couple of eggs we're eating look like identical twins, and they're not even third cousins.

—GOMEZ DE LA SERNA

This morning's donuts are now hard and cynical.

–DAN LIEBERT

But writers quickly pushed de la Serna's gregueria down their own paths, even going so far as to oppose his instruction and make them sad:

Loneliest of all is the bubble in a spirit level.

–DAN LIEBERT

Or stark and silent:

In the village church the saints have forgotten all about God and are watching the snow fall.

–CHARLES SIMIC

These improvisations on the gregueria seem like lines

kidnapped from poems and left to live alone. They leave the reader not with didactic knowledge or even a new insight, but with a mental image and its piquant feeling. Insight from a gregueria is connotative, much like what we get from haiku.

The Irish Bull

In addition to greguerias, there's the perversely entertaining Irish Bull. As Samuel Taylor Coleridge so aptly described it, "The bull consists in the bringing together of two incompatible thoughts, with the *sensation*, but without the *sense*, of their connection."

I refuse to join any club that would have me as a member.

—GROUCHO MARX

It is a sobering thought that when Mozart was my age, he had been dead for two years. —TOM LEHRER

How does an Irish bull work differently than a run-of-the-mill aphoristic twist? In a traditional aphorism, once the dust from its surprise settles, we're left with a clear statement. But the twist in a bull, unlike the twist in an aphorism, just keeps twisting. It defies clear meaning, tantalizing the reader. The two thoughts juxtaposed seem logically absurd, but some part of us hopes that if we let the sensation linger – if we allow it to press against our need for clarity – then something resembling a truth might shake out like a potato from a burlap bag. An Irish bull is always pregnant with a meaning it never delivers.

Appropriately, no one's sure how people started using the term *bull* this way. It may be named after a 13th Century Irish lawyer, Obidiah Bull. Or it might derive from Old French *boule*, meaning fraud, deceit, or trickery. Or, in thoroughly Modern English: *bullshit*. And what about the Irish part?

The aphoristic form seems Irish in at least one other way. It could be a cousin to other Celtic intricacies like contrapuntal fiddle music, the manic labyrinthine spirals in the *Book of Kells* and the triple puns in *Finnegan's Wake*. With bulls, the madness comes in knotting opposite ideas together in a way both absurd and yet, yet . . .

Sometimes I can't tell myself apart.

Or long-form ambiguity:

The red-headed boy looks at the penny. "Heads," he says, "is better than tails."

"No," the dark-haired boy states flatly. "Tails is better."

Suddenly a little girl wearing overalls appears. She snatches up the penny and feeds it into a gumball machine. Down comes the bright orange gumball, and she pops it in her mouth.

"Yum," she says and walks away, leaving the boys penniless.

Whether you take your truths straight or with a twist, we hope *Short Flights* will deliver you many moments of surprise, joy, insight, outrage and bewilderment. It did us.

Those who are easily shocked should be shocked more often.

—MAE WEST

Aphorisms

James Richardson

In 1993, I was looking in Montaigne for help with an essay to be called "On Likeness." A footnote sent me to the maxims of La Rochefoucauld, which I read not only with delight but with something like ricochet. "Wait, that's not right," I'd mutter, or "That's not *all*," scribbling some correction or analogue or sequel to one of his insights. My response often felt like a flipping or twisting of the Duc's sentences, a spatial skill not dissimilar from those involved in making metaphors, doing math and solving various small household problems.

Actually I should have said "my responses," since often I'd end up with many slightly different versions of the same aphorism. They came so quickly that it felt more like reading than writing. Good Taste would later have to choose which version worked. I thought of them as isomers – chemical compounds which have the same formula but may differ utterly in their properties because they are different shapes.

No one will ever write a novel by accident. A poem, too, takes time. But if I say "Pick a word" and you say one, where did it come from? You certainly don't say you "wrote it" or "created it" – more like you chose it, or it chose you. One-liners must be in the middle of that spectrum, as much accident as composition. Almost all Proverbs and most of the jokes that make the rounds are anonymous: who came up with them, and how? I feel that way about some of my aphorisms, as if couldn't claim authorship. I do anyway, but I have a soft spot for the ones that sound most like proverbs written by no one, short and unsophisticated, their reference restricted to nature and household:

Snakes cannot back up.

Nothing dirtier than old soap.

All stones are broken stones.

Probably in looking back I've exaggerated the automatism and impersonality of the form, but it is really true that "I" seem to me the greatest danger to my work.

Still, some aphorisms I claim not only as mine but as me. "All work is the avoidance of harder work" and "The best time is stolen time" are something like personal mottoes, and I also think of them privately as *about* writing aphorisms. What has by now become hundreds of aphorisms feels to me like a long procrastination, a parenthesis in that essay on metaphor that I started writing in 1993 . . . and still haven't finished.

• • •

The road reaches every place, the short cut only one.

Of all the ways to avoid living, perfect discipline is the most admired.

If you're Larkin or Bishop, one book a decade is enough. If you're not? More than enough.

The will is weak. Good thing, or we'd succeed in governing our lives with our stupid ideas!

Once it's gone, how easy to say it was mine.

In clearing out files, ideas, hopes, throw away a little too much. Pruning only dead wood will not encourage growth.

God help my neighbors if I loved them as I love myself.

You can't pretend you're just watching the actors. Someone a little further away will see you acting the part of a watcher.

Success repeats itself until it is failure.

Despair says *It's all the same.* Happiness can distinguish a thousand Despairs.

Those who are too slow to be intelligent deserve our patience, those who are too quick, our pity.

Think of all the smart people made stupid by flaws of character. The finest watch isn't fine long when used as a hammer.

Only the dead have discovered what they cannot live without.

Even at the movies, we laugh together, we weep alone.

If the saints are perfect and unwavering we are excused from trying to imitate them. Also if they are not.

Everyone loves the Revolution. We only disagree on whether it has occurred.

No price fluctuates so wildly as that of time.

To be sincere is one thing. To practice Sincerity is to burden everyone else with believing you.

No matter how fast you travel, life walks.

The future is pure luck. But once it arrives it begins to seem explainable. Not long afterwards, it could hardly have happened otherwise.

A tornado can't stack two dimes.

Water deepens where it has to wait.

It's amazing that I sit at my job all day and no one sees me clearly enough to say *What is that boy doing behind a desk?*

Who breaks the thread, the one who pulls, the one who holds on?

There are only three subjects: death, love and justice. All of them are depicted as blind.

There are silences harder to take back than words.

For one who needs it, praise is pity.

Ax built the house but sleeps in the shed.

The road you do not take you will have to cross.

As with bacteria, so with troubles. They evolve resistance to our cures.

The water cannot talk without the rocks.

I was 25 till I was 40, 40 till I was 50. But now my age is like the speedometer. If I don't pay attention it drifts, 60, 70, 80 ...

A beginning ends what an end begins.

Each lock makes two prisons.

The world is not what anyone wished for, it's what everyone wished for.

Wind cannot blow the wind away, nor water wash away the water.

We do not love money. But once we have it, it is not money – it is ours.

The ruts are deepest in the middle of the road.

The first abuse of power is not realizing that you have it.

Money and love both say they are all you need.

I sell my time to get enough money to buy it back.

Beware of knowing your virtues; you may lose them. Beware of knowing your vices; you may forgive them.

Debts of a certain immensity demand betrayal.

If you say *All is well*, I believe you. If I say *All is well*, I'm abbreviating.

Experience is being a little surer of what won't ever happen.

We are never so aware of how we look to others as when we have a great secret. Vanity always thinks it has a great secret.

The ambitious: those who have to work longer to find a place where it seems safe to stop.

Minds go from intuition to articulation to self-defense, which is what they die of.

Believe in everything a little. The credulous know things the skeptical do not.

The hardest thing to allow my child is my mistakes.

Charles Simic

Form is "timing" – the exact amount of silence necessary between words and images to make them meaningful. The stand-up comedians know all about that.

If I make everything at the same time a joke and a serious matter, it's because I honor the eternal conflict between life and art, the absolute and the relative, the brain and the belly, etc… No philosophy is good enough to overcome a toothache … that sort of thing.

I'd like to show readers that the most familiar things that surround them are unintelligible. Form is not a "shape" but an "image," the way in which my inwardness seeks visibility.

How to communicate consciousness… the present moment lived intensely that language locked in the temporal order of the sentence cannot reproduce?

Metaphor offers the opportunity for my inwardness to connect itself with the world out there.

All things are related, and that knowledge resides in my unconscious.

• • •

What a mess! I believe in images of transcendence, but I don't believe in God!

The inventor of the modern metaphor, Arthur Rimbaud, regarded himself as a seer. He saws that the secret ambition of a radical metaphor is metaphysical. It could open new worlds. It could touch the absolute. He gave up poetry when he began to doubt that truth.

Truth is known at precisely that point in time when nobody gives a shit.

Everything of course is a mirror if you look at it long enough.

To be an exception to the rule is my sole ambition.

Anywhere conformity is an ideal, poetry is not welcome.

I don't believe in God but I'm afraid of opening an umbrella in the house.

The attentive eye begins to hear.

Imagination equals Eros.

How do we know the other? By being madly in love.

Every poetic image asks why there is something rather than nothing.

Intense experience eludes language.

The beauty of a fleeting moment is eternal.

The farther the injustice, the louder the outrage.

He who cannot howl will not find his pack.

Serenity is the outside appearance of lucidity.

Silence is the only language God speaks.

Awe is my religion and mystery its church.

The snow grows whiter after a crow has flown over it.

The kindness of one human being to another in times of mass hatred and violence deserves more respect than the preaching of all the churches since the beginning of time.

Religion: Turning the mystery of Being into a figure who resembles our grandfather sitting on the potty.

The new American Dream is to get to be very rich and still be regarded as a victim.

Every nation is scared of the truth of what they have done to others.

The chief role of a free press in democracy is to conceal that the country is ruled by a few.

The soul is a shadow cast by the light of consciousness. In the meantime, I can feel a sneeze coming.

The servants of the rich and powerful are convinced that the rest of us envy them their servitude.

The imagination has moments when it knows what the word "infinity" means.

Beware of synchronicity – "the meaningful coincidence of an external event with an inner motive." That way madness lies.

Being is not an idea in philosophy, but a wordless experience we have from time to time.

One mad idea after another let loose upon the world as if they were soap bubbles and we small children running after them.

Finally a just war; all the innocents killed in it can regard themselves as lucky.

He reads the papers with mounting satisfaction that everything is going to hell, just as he predicted.

Another century in which anyone who thought deeply found himself alone and speechless.

Greguerias

My insomnia: an iceberg split from infinity's Pole.

He could read the mind of a lit match as it entered a dark room.

In the village church the saints have forgotten all about God and are watching the snow fall.

The infinite riches of an empty room.

Eternity is the insomnia of Time.

James Lough

It would be nice to say I took to writing aphorisms because I felt like I had something to *say*, something sinewy and deep that would lodge itself in readers' minds and open up their lives. It would also be nice to say I was a natural wit like Oscar Wilde, scandalizing high society's dinner table with subversive apercus over aperitifs.

The truth is I took up aphorisms because of a broken condom. My wife and I had one more kid than we planned, then *two* more kids (call us irresponsible). On top of that, a new and demanding teaching job was feeding me stacks of 80 papers to grade every few weeks. With two male toddlers trundling into my office, crawling over my desk as I tried to mark run-on-sentences – not to mention a baby girl on the way – I just didn't have time. The longer forms I used to work in – stories, essays, novels – required me to sit and concentrate at the computer for hours at a stretch.

"There is no more somber enemy of good art than the pram in the hall," wrote Cyril Connolly. When I was a childless free agent, his aphorism delighted me as much as it now irks. My only revenge is to say that Connolly, the bachelor, never managed to write the great novel he felt destined to. It's a lukewarm *touché*.

Nevertheless, short on time to write, I had to write short. While I loved poetry, I had never felt the talent or tug to "tell it slant." My aim was to lunge straight at the subject, like a philosopher swinging a butterfly net at insights fanning their wings through mind's blue sky, then pinning them down to examine. I had always kept a little notepad in my pocket for scribbling ideas, fragments, and impressions - bits I might later slip into longer works to flesh them out. Now those ideas, fragments and impressions have become the final products.

• • •

Aphorism: a little window with a big view.

Buddhism: Much ado about nothingness.

Death: The night at the end of the tunnel.

Intelligence: the ability in other people to see things your way.

Perfection: a fleeting byproduct of miraculous luck. The more one reaches for it, the farther it recedes.

Religion: a dead monument to a living truth.

Virtue: a practice that keeps you out of debt, prison, and country clubs.

A clenched fist in flowing water – that is what we are.

Nothing is as earnest as unhappiness.

It's all relative? Absolutely.

He doesn't need imagination – he's got money.

We say knowledge is power, we celebrate charisma as power, but both perform poorly next to the power of money.

We rankle at the opinions we most recently outgrew.

The insomniac ponders death. *At least I'd get some rest.*

Should we wonder why our kids are confused? In the car we tell them to sit down and buckle up. At school we tell them to sit up and buckle down.

If God is everything and everywhere, then even God must occasionally doubt He exists.

In life, as in bicycling, pedal when you have to, coast when you can.

Next time get it right the first time.

Time is money, but only one of them is sure to run out.

Few of us want to be elitists – but we're okay with being elites.

Misery is never getting what you want. There are two ways around this – setting out to get it all, or limiting your wants. One is futile, the other hopeless.

Blame the limits of language? First check the limits of the writer.

What a romantic calls an outrage, a realist sees as more of the same.

It travels at the speed of lies.

There's no truth in *I was just asking* and no point to *I'm just saying.*

The ultimate power, the power beyond all powers, is the power of indifference.

Here now
Now here
Nowhere

Another day, another dolor.

It's easy to be a sadist. Now being a masochist, that takes balls.

To get your way, you must finesse your foes. Your friends you can force.

The portal, the door, the sewage hole to the Infinite.

Finding where you fit in, you no longer need to stand out.

It's safer to dislike something than admit you don't understand it.

Ah, the innocence of children! Even their cruelty is innocent.

We're doing the best we can. That's the problem.

If effing is short for fucking, does ineffable mean it can't be fucked?

Get with the program, they say. Which really means *Get with the programming*.

In the USA, the idea that we use only 10% of our brains means we could be 90% richer.

Someone who is whole is not pure. Someone who is pure is not whole. You get to decide.

Foodies and the homeless have one thing in common: it's all about the next meal.

Excess opportunities morph into obstacles – wishes fulfilled become obligations.

The more stuff you have, the more stuff you have to do.

Inspirational messages always say Dream.
What if they said Work?

No fair spreading Miracle-Gro on the lilies of the field.

The most grandiose, sophisticated moral theories are all variations on a simple theme: do no harm.

Our periodic table lays out 118 elements. But the chemists ignore my letters and won't add the element of surprise.

It's not the heat, it's the humanity.

I'm anxiously awaiting the response to a text message I haven't yet sent.

How to love your enemies: first make enemies.

Grandparents and grandchildren get along so well because they share a common enemy.

That's why God gave us satire.

Sara Levine

I can't pack light; I bring too many sweaters.

I can't cook light either. Last week I invited one person to dinner and made three entrees.

It's also true, as the slow warm-up of this sentence suggests, that I can't tell a story quickly. ("Too many prefaces!" say friends.) Recently my husband, who was driving us downtown, seemed, all at once, to require warning about an oncoming vehicle. I panicked, shunning the brief, effective, time-honored shout – "Look out!" – in favor of something along the lines of, "I could be wrong about this, but ..." By the time I finished my sentence, he had averted the accident and eaten up another mile of the road.

I long to be minimal, but something about me is maximal. I *tell* people I'm a neat freak, but on the counter beside me now there lie a bag of birdseed, a bowl of grapes, three unmailed letters, two sets of earphones, the check that should have been cashed yesterday, a bowl of dried-up limes, four books, three binder clips, and a large square piece of green foam. (Whose foam *is* that? What's it even *for*?)

Maybe I like the aphorism because it goads me to overcome excess. I can't keep the menu simple or the luggage light or the counter clean, but since I can keep a sentence brief, it frequently seems right to do so.

• • •

I tend to choose narcissists as my friends; that way I don't worry that they're talking about me behind my back.

I can give you my psychology in a nutshell: me inside a nutshell, listening for the nutcracker's approach.

My mother gave birth to me once, yeah yeah yeah. But I've redone myself a million times.

Why do women write so few aphorisms? he asked me. Why do men write so many?

I found her remarks so appalling I did my best to sustain the friendship. Not because I enjoyed her, but because I enjoyed my capacity to be appalled.

The financial facts of life are like certain acquaintances; I only greet them if it's impossible to duck into a doorway.

Can you be joyed? Or only overjoyed?

I never judge other mothers, even when they're doing everything wrong.

I learned to forgive his faults – and then, more happily, to forgive his faults in another friend's presence. I don't want to simply forbear; I want to be known as forbearing.

Willpower is like Jesus; it dies so it can be resurrected.

"How can I thank you? Tell me how to thank you."
No, you figure out how to thank me. Haven't I done enough?

And they lived less unhappily than other people ever after.

Sharon Dolin

The liberal sense of what an aphorism can be – sometimes philosophical, psychological, self-reflective, diaristic, observational, linked – is a form I first felt drawn to when traveling with my family in Greece. How to steal time for writing when I was in the midst of marital discord and a demanding 8-year-old. The aphorism, that brief slice of air, was my solution.

The spirit of place has shaped my aphorisms, as well as my proclivity to write them in a sequence – where they build upon each other – as opposed to plucking isolated nuggets from life's tree. This is an unusual way to write aphorisms but I am interested in expanding the notion of what an aphorism can be: from a pithy saying; to an image or personal thought; to an entire sequence of thoughts, images, and sayings.

My project in writing these aphoristic sequences is to expand/challenge received (alas, male) notions of aphorisms as crystalline, impersonal truths. An aphorism can be personal and not generic – as so many good aphorisms are. I am interested in the space – the seam, as in stitching – where the lyric and the aphorism meet and marry.

The reason aphorisms fell out of favor is the same

reason why women don't usually write them. Traditionally, they have dressed themselves in the suit of rhetorical authority – and since the Sixties, relativism, the personal, the subjective, has been the only acceptable truth. Have we now reached the limit of the local truth and will there now be a renewed interest in the aphorism but with a more particular nuanced, personal voice?

Let Edmond Jabès, grand master of the aphorism as spiritual autobiography, speak for my project to renovate the aphorism from the impersonal to the personal:

"To introduce autobiography into a Jewish text [substitute 'aphorism'], to rehabilitate the I – the particular that gives rise to the universal – to insist on the face and then proceed slowly to wipe out this insistence."

(THE BOOK OF SHARES)

• • •

From *Istanbul Diary*

Aryan (sounds like eiron): yogurt drink at every meal. Daily theater of the pour.

In the end, it all comes down to thirst.

Most erotic, least expected.

My twin shrines of memory: his hand reaching
into the back of my skirt. His tongue pulling on my
tongue.

Metaphor conquers pain.

If the lyric poem's motto is still *Show don't tell*,
the lover's request is *Take me, don't ask..*

Tacit assent to being ravished is still being ravished.

Joyce got female desire wrong. Saying *No* is always
more erotic than saying *Yes*.

In love play, the one holding down is really the one
being held down.

English is my burkah; Turkish, theirs.

Passing stands of cypresses: the long green fingers of the landscape waving hands.

Chilies drying on the line – Turkish necklaces of the poor.

Old woman on the road. Back bent. Nothing left to carry but her life.

Accidents are gifts of transformation. Or deformation.

To shake her and dare him: what "Thank you" sounds like in Turkish.

The artist performs a special kind of photosynthesis:
Like the sunflower, first she creates a tall flashy flower
that then grows heavy with seeds whose small hard
shells you must crack to get to the rich nut meat.

There may be no progress in art, but if the artist does
not metamorphose within each work, the art will die and
be scattered for hogs like ears of unripened corn. This
too is the true soul of each of us.

Must lovers metamorphose as well?

How much more difficult it becomes to value the
pearl when you find its gleam within the first oyster
you dive for and split open.

Like the Canaanites wandering in the desert for a
single day and being given the law with all that flash
and thunder.

From *Andalusian Wind*

Looking for scorpions: What we fear most is what we most want to see.

If you keep straining to see what shape your life is taking, it will take the shape of your straining body.

Mojácar's beach in May is so deserted even your loneliness lacks company.

Pendant lemons. The breasts of Mojácar.

Medlar in a net to keep the birds away – like the ringing of his unanswered phone to fence his heart.

The aphorist assumes that small truths can be packed into a sentence the way the olive packs its fruit around the pit.

What if I have gone to a place where the truths I am searching for are like the fruit trees behind barbed wire. Or are the barbed wire.

Or the hand-hewn stone walls that invite and repel.

All those artists who say they are not in search of the truth have merely given up thema for anathema – which is a different kind of truth. As the writers proclaiming the death of the author always sign their books.

Anguish: that the present is consumed with reliving – refiguring – the past as a way to figure out the future. All futile. All dead letters.

So many wind turbines (at first I wrote turbans) on the hillsides on the way to Granada: enormous white-winged birds with several long, energetic, spinning tails for spinning out dreams against the blue sky.

So many dried-out riverbeds. So many exhausted metaphors.

How many days have you spent never once taking in the air that stirs your hair, the bird song that laces through your thoughts.

What does it mean to be an artist: to be a scavenger of the overlooked.

Still life artists are the truest to their calling because they raise up the ordinary and say, "This!"

H.L. Hix

I had to bluff my way through graduate school, primarily because I was a stumbling student but also because the longer I studied in my field (philosophy) the farther I moved toward its margins. My weakness as a student (which I have *tried* at least to diminish over time) and my marginality as a philosopher (which has only increased) – meet at various points.One of them is my affinity for the aphorism.

In a seminar I struggled through on the Presocratics (struggled because the other students all had better Greek than mine, and better backgrounds in the ancients), I wanted to tender gratitude for the professor's sympathy and patience by showing him I was working hard, even though my research paper wasn't going to advance scholarship on the subject. My strategy was to create, in lieu of the "normal" paper for which I was inadequately prepared, a new arrangement of the fragments of Heraclitus: proof I was earnest enough to struggle with the material even though I wasn't smart enough to arrive at some keen insight that might hold value for others. Reflecting on that project now, I can confirm that it *didn't* offer any insight to others, but working intensively in that way with Heraclitus' fragments – his aphorisms – did lend me some insight.

That project helped me coalesce some intuitions I felt pulling me against the current of my program of study. The program was heavily analytical, but Heraclitus helped me see that it was *synthesis* more than analysis that I admired, and synthesis I sought. *Hen to sophon*, Heraclitus (de) claims: the wise is one. The only required course in an otherwise wholly elective curriculum was symbolic logic, but even then I sensed that syllogism was neither the sole nor the soul path to apprehension. I wished for something much more like gestalt. The program took for granted that the proper philosophical approach to the world, and to one's life, is argument, whose final aim is truth. I found myself seeking to approach the world and my life through awe, which takes as ultimate not truth but mystery. The program valued statement, reference, denotation; I valued implication, sense, connotation.

I saw all these intuitions concentrated into the aphoristic form, that of Heraclitus and Nietzsche and Wittgenstein, and that of its newer sources as Antonio Porchia, Jan Zwicky and Elias Canetti. Instead of the more standard nominal form, *truth*, used as the goal of reasoning, the point at which it would stop, I heard in the aphorism its more compelling verb form, *to true* (as in to true a wheel) an ongoing activity that ought not end. I didn't want to subject emotion to reason, or to subject desire to disinterestedness, but to true each by the other. I saw the aphorism as a catalyst for those pursuits.

• • •

Most writers write only books they have read, and most readers read only books they would write.

Read 1000 books. Befriend 100. Know 10 by heart. Write 1.

Ideas arrive like meteors, not like doves. The force of the impact lasts, not the idea itself, and not the reasoning that follows after.

Like a gas, like language, god expands to fill the space provided.

Better to make angels (we have too few) than gods (we have too many).

Fall on one's knees, or be driven to them.

Thought matters as passion, passion matters as discipline, discipline matters as courage, courage matters as beauty, beauty matters as sorrow, sorrow matters as thought.

Art changes the geometry of the world, draws us to the edge where the unimagined falls into the unimaginable.

The artist counts stars through the holes in the ceiling while falling through a hole in the floor.

That extinct totem animal, truth: reason specifies where it would be found if it still existed, and art describes what the animal would look like if you could get there.

People think the indictments they make come from god, as cats think all that moves is alive.

Even about suffering we are intolerant: you
must suffer my way. I permit only torments I can
understand, only what would torment a person like
myself.

A mind full of birds helps only one who can fly.

Only the ability to starve ourselves distinguishes us
from flies seething above a carcass.

Our inability to entertain a multiplicity of ideas
simultaneously, we call "truth."

Delphi did not become an oracle because its
prophecies were true; its prophecies came true
because it was an oracle.

Like words, ideas combine.

Belief suffocates imagination.

Distance and darkness limit, but do not impoverish, vision.

The blind, sessile anemone knows the reef well enough.

I can name everything I have given up, nothing I have not.

Of ideas, too, there are hunter/gatherers, farmers, and merchants.

In seeking the river's source, twenty minutes' rest undoes an hour's labor, as the current draws one back to sea.

The parrot's colors still flame in the cage, but to what end?

History began with us, led to us, will end with us: three masks for one mistake.

Humans, the animals whose primary parasites belong to their own species.

How tempting to transform mysteries into truths, but the true remains so by being left out of all accounts.

Nostalgia occurs when affection for some past self overcomes the will to create a new one.

Our finitude: we can trade one self for another, but not trade back.

There are only minor prophets. To be heard more widely, one would need to commit the sins against which prophets speak.

Beauty thrives, like anaerobic bacteria or ocean-floor tubeworms, even in the absence of apparent preconditions for life.

Minds, stars suspended in space by attraction to other stars.

Ashleigh Brilliant

Ashleigh Brilliant is my real name. But, although I am in fact a Life Member of MENSA, there is only one truly brilliant achievement to which I lay claim.

I always wanted to be a writer, but early in life I became aware that the field was overcrowded. "To be sure of winning" (as one of my lines says) "invent your own game, and never tell any other player the rules." So I invented my own writing game. I did however take the risk of proclaiming these rules, which I call Pot-Shots or Brilliant Thoughts.

The length limit is 17 words. That is a maximum. There is no minimum.

They must be easy to translate into other languages, and easily understood in other times and places – hence no rhyme, rhythm, idioms, puns, or other kinds of word-play, also, no topical or cultural references.

Each epigram must be as different as possible from anything known to have ever been uttered before by anyone.

Whatever is expressed must be really worth saying, and said as well as possible.

Although illustrations may be supplied, none is required for the meaning to be appreciated.

In view of that last point, you may be interested to know that back in 1964, towards the end of my long grind as a graduate student of History at Berkeley, I decided to see if I could make a living, not as a writer but as an artist. I produced a batch of paintings, all of either a surrealistic or a totally abstract nature – and displayed them in a few local shows. This experiment taught me a valuable lesson, which led on to my subsequent career as an epigrammatist. I observed that some people were more impressed with the *titles* which I wrote at the bottom than with the art – even to the point of sometimes buying the picture for the sake of the words. Evidently, very short expressions could have both literary and commercial value.

With that in mind, I began making lists of possible titles for future art-works. Then it occurred to me that these could be regarded as a kind of one-line poetry, and I started reciting them at parties. People would say "you ought to publish those." I wanted to emphasize that each one was a separate work, so in 1967, I began printing and distributing them as postcards, in a series which now totals 10,000 different messages. And since this genre can readily be applied to all kinds of objects, spaces, and surfaces, I soon found myself branching out into syndication, books, T-shirts, and any number of other licensed products.

One thing which has made my work distinct has been a resolute insistence upon copyrighting every line separately, and doing anything necessary to protect them against infringement. This, I felt, was the only way to attain my true objective: literary and academic respectability, as ultimately embodied, perhaps, in the Nobel Prize for Literature.

Considering the distinguished company among which I find myself here, my inclusion in this book can be regarded as at least a modest step towards that goal – for which I wish sincerely to thank the Editors.

...

The reasons for my existence have not yet been established, but investigation is continuing.

Due to circumstances beyond my control, I am master of my fate and captain of my soul.

Obviously there's a big difference between right and wrong. The only slight problem is: which is which?

Sometimes I think I understand everything – then I regain consciousness.

I could not possibly imagine a world like this, so it must be real.

I'm living the best life I can, in case it turns out to be my only one.

Either this life I'm in is very dream-like, or this dream I'm in is very life-like.

At least we're all free to choose the inevitable.

There's only one everything.

I find it easier to be a result of the past than a cause of the future.

What makes the universe so hard to comprehend is that there's nothing to compare it with.

If everything is part of a whole, what is the whole part of?

Life may have no meaning, or, even worse, it may have a meaning of which I disapprove.

Life is the only game in which the object of the game is to learn the rules.

Nothing we can do can change the past, but every-thing we do changes the future.

Prove to me, if you can, that, after I die, the world will still exist.

It's all very simple, or else it's all very complex, or perhaps it's neither, or both.

History clearly shows that people come and people go, but, beyond that, nothing else is very clear.

I wish somebody would expose me for what I really am, so that I would know.

In the final analysis, life may be meaningless, but, fortunately, the final analysis hasn't yet been made.

It troubles me that I have no way of knowing what I have no way of knowing.

I've learned to accept birth and death, but sometimes I still worry about what lies between.

The truth is that I really don't know what the truth is.

What exactly is life? I need to know before I can make any important decisions.

If God knew I would lose anyway, why did he make me try so hard to win?

Which version of the truth would you like to be told today?

Yahia Lababidi

I first began experimenting with silence in university. I would go on fasts for day at a time, rationing words, and speaking only when I must. Friends understood that I'd 'gone under' and only the very committed continued to leave me voice messages or, braver still, tagged along, noiselessly.

The idea at the time – more inner imperative, really, than any sort of formulated thought – was to sound my depths and think things through. This was my first taste of freedom as an adult, and that is how I chose to exercise it. It was as though, suddenly and without explanation, I was taken in for questioning, and I had to play both parts: officer and suspect. *Who was I, What did I know, Why am I here,* and *Do I have an alibi?*

Typically, I'd walk around all day in a semi-trance talking back to the books I'd read, lost in the echo chamber of my head. I read a great deal more those days, again out of an inner imperative, but hardly the assigned work. My self-imposed reading list was a volatile cocktail, unequal parts literature/philosophy, and the discovery of those great contrarians, Wilde and Nietzsche, made my world spin faster. Unaware of it then, this obsessive reading was in fact teaching me how to write. The rhythms and cadences of my literary Masters insinuated themselves into my style, just as their stances and daring were persuading me to distrust ready-made ideas and try to articulate better questions.

It was out of these silences and (attendant) solitude that I began writing what would become my first book of aphorisms – by transcribing the heady conversations that I was having with myself at the time. My 'method' in writing these aphorisms was simply to jot down on a scrap of paper (the back of a napkin, receipt, or whatever else was handy) what I thought was worth quoting from the soul's dialogue with itself.

If ever I tried keeping a notebook, the thoughts would hesitate leaving their cave – sensing ambush. So, by night I kept bits of paper and a pencil by my side, just in case. And, when something did occur to me, I feverishly scribbled it down in the dark, without my glasses, out of the same superstitious cautiousness of scaring ideas off.

These aphorisms were to reveal me to myself and would serve as the biography of my mental, spiritual and emotional life. I read as I wrote, helplessly, in a state of emergency; and, in my youthful fanaticism, I was convinced that I was squeezing existence for answers, no less. I felt then one should only read on a need-to-know basis, and write discriminatingly, with the sole purpose of intensifying consciousness.

Which is to say, I composed the bulk of the aphorisms in my book, *Signposts to Elsewhere*, between the improbable ages of 18-21.

• • •

Impulses we attempt to strangle only develop stronger muscles.

The small spirit is quick to misperceive an insult, the large spirit is slow to receive a compliment.

Time heals old wounds only because there are new wounds to attend to.

A good listener helps us overhear ourselves.

Envious of natural disasters, men create their own.

Spiritually occurs at the boiling point of religion, where dogma evaporates.

Pleasure may be snatched from life's clenched fists, not joy.

We are no more related to our past selves than we are to our future selves.

To be treated with mercy, some of us must reveal our handicaps, others must conceal theirs.

Truth can be like a large, bothersome fly – brush it away and it returns buzzing.

With enigmatic clarity, Life gives us a different answer each time we ask her the same question.

Things are at their most comfortable before they collapse – be they armchairs or relationships.

Alienation: the crippling conviction that one is a minority of one.

Ambiguity: the bastard child of creativity and cowardice.

Arrogance: the vain, younger sister of confidence.

Chemical warfare: psychiatry's answer to the battlefield of the mind.

Contradictions: the curse of the clever.

Despair: an early surrender, where the spirit dies before the body does.

Discipline: the backbone without which potential cannot stand.

Dreams: what get us through the night, and oftentimes the day.

Hope: the refusal to accept things as they are.

Ideals: maps that omit practical details – like mountain ranges.

Liar: one who claims to tell the truth, always.

Life: a midway point between two unknowns.

Morality: only permitting others to behave as we behave, when we behave.

Nostalgia: the familiar pinch of that outgrown garment.

Religion: faith in a harness.

Self-consciousness: a weed in the garden of self-awareness.

Self-image: Self-deception.

Uncertainty: the starting and ending point of Knowledge.

War: the side-effect of nationalism.

Brian Jay Stanley

I write aphorisms because they suit the variety of life. The world is too rich for me to have a long attention span; I can scarcely settle my thoughts to read long books, let alone write them. One event follows another, each of them interesting, and I would comment on all of them. Since I cannot write a book about everything, I write an aphorism.

Writing aids my attention to life, because writing requires clear thoughts and close observations. I seek a thousand small truths. My one big truth is that the details of life are inexhaustibly fascinating.

I like aphorisms for the same reason I like poetry: they distill lucidity and meaning from the vague profundity of experience. But whereas poetry targets the senses and feelings, aphorisms target the mind. Aphorisms are the philosopher's version of poetry.

I am drawn to the staying power of aphorisms, their potential to be as relevant in the future as in the present. I could never be a journalist, laboring over articles which readers will toss in the recycling bin tomorrow. Desiring an audience, I would not limit my pool of potential readers to people now living. What if the right reader of my words has not yet been born? The daydream that my writing might outlive me nourishes my labor; the hope for future readers compensates the paucity of present ones.

Thoughts of time and mortality fuel my desire to write quotable sentences. If I can make readers adopt a few of my words into memory, I gain an afterlife in their brains. The secret meaning of every aphorism is, *do not forget me*.

· · ·

Human nature needs both fellowship and freedom, but usually we must choose. The more we encircle ourselves with others, the more we handcuff our will. Ask for help on a project at work, and it will not be done exactly how you want. Marry, and your holidays will be spent at in-laws'. Have children, and you will listen to their music in the car instead of yours. But worship your freedom, and you will be an empty temple. A bachelor's life resembles a widower's. Write, sing, or paint the way you please, disregarding the market's demands, and you will be your own and only audience. Travel wherever you want, whenever you want, and you will go alone.

Fellowship imprisons us, freedom exiles us.

During campaign seasons, I tire of the candidates' attack ads and mutual rummaging through one another's past sins. Such faultfinding, most of it false or exaggerated, seems not only mean-spirited but also petty and immature, like children too eager to tattle. One expects rudeness from taxi drivers or football fans, but not from men and women seeking the highest offices of government. Are these self-promoting finger-pointers to be the leaders of nations? But then I remember the old days, when would-be kings, backed by armies instead of campaign teams, rode out to bloody battles, took their rival's children captive, and cut off each other's head to gain the crown. From murder and kidnap, to mere lies and slander. Civilization is making progress.

The poverty line has risen throughout history. The tenants of modern trailer parks live in more luxury than early Sumerian aristocrats, whose mansions were reed huts with dirt floors. The motor scooters of unemployed college students travel faster than the horses of medieval lords. Civil War generals communicated by courier, but now every private has a mobile phone. Progress impoverishes the past. Complaints lose power when you think of your ancestors. We decry the cost of health insurance, but a century ago, there existed neither health insurance nor cures for it to pay for. I grumble when my air conditioning breaks in summer, but in ancient Egypt even Pharaohs had to sweat.

The problem with visiting historic cities is that we can only go in the present. Drawn by a magnificent past, we arrive to the deflating realization that this place which was once a stage is now a backwater. What greatness has issued from Florence in the last

four centuries? I do not so much want to visit Florence, but to visit the Renaissance; I do not want to see
Michelangelo's paintings, but Michelangelo painting.
I would like to pick a century as well as a country
when I travel.

Having felt let down visiting history's has-beens,
I prefer places whose moment is now. One travels to
Hong Kong or San Francisco not for what they were,
but what they are. San Francisco was a sand dune
when Brunelleschi was building his dome and the
Medici ousted Machiavelli, but now history ships
from Silicon Valley while storied Florence is reduced
to reminiscence. The best place to look for life is in
the present, and in imagination of the past. Thus I read
books about Florence, and book flights to California.

When I look at my wedding photo, I am amazed that
such an important decision as whom to spend my
life with was made by someone so young. The life I
live now, albeit happily, is not the life that I, but this
baby face, chose. With age we get wiser, but our
green and innocent selves have already made life's
great decisions. A doctor labors for forty years at a
career he chose as a college sophomore. A fifty-year
old smokes because a fifteen-year old wanted to
try it. Decision is brief, and consequence long. Five
minutes of pleasure leads to parenthood. Moments
determine decades.

When I see nature bulldozed to build subdivisions, I feel anger toward the developers. But when I drive by later and see the new homes filled with families, my anger goes flaccid. Must not the families live somewhere? True, they had homes before, but those homes now house others, and the others' old homes house others too. Trace the trail of new construction back to its origin, and you arrive at a hospital maternity ward humming like a factory day and night, sending endless swaddled shipments of future homebuyers into the world. Developers build because parents beget. Suburbs sprawl because lovers do.

The busier I get, the more barren my life seems of meaning, but the less time I have to worry about it. Galloping to keep up with my calendar, tripping over appointments, occasionally I glimpse the absurdity of the frantic life. The only purpose of today is to check off yesterday's to-do list, and create tomorrow's. My overscheduled mind scarcely stops to let me sleep, yet my thoughts add up to mindlessness, since I never pause to notice I am living. Am I only a machine for labor, a thinking version of an ox?

Luckily, my vision of existential futility is cut short by my next approaching deadline. Busyness is the cause, and the cure, of a pointless life.

Success, by way of ambition, leads to failure. The more we achieve, the more we think we can achieve; our hopes rise exponentially in relation to our skill. Talented drama students, heartened by the cheers of local audiences, journey to Hollywood after high school, where everyone was a talented drama student, and there are only jobs as extras. The best baseball players in the minor league go to the major league, where they are the worst players. As air bubbles rise through water and dissolve in the atmosphere, the above average rise until they are average. As we ascend the ranks, our status falls.

Dan Liebert

' **G**regueria' is the creation and lifelong obsession of Spanish writer, Ramon Gomez de la Serna, (1888-1963). It combines aphoristic assertion, the punchline 'kick' of a one-line joke, and a child-like delight in metaphor. If I am the world's only publishing writer of the 'gregueria,' I say it more out of loneliness than pride.

This, by Ramon, is everything a fine gregueria should be:

Water lets her hair down in waterfalls.

Women of 1910 wore their hair piled high on their heads and only 'let it down' in the intimacy of the boudoir. Waist length hair was the norm and even ankle-length not uncommon. We can scarcely imagine the erotic intensity of this 'hair-fall' moment for a bourgeois gentleman of Ramon's youth.

The 'sense' of a gregueria must be immediate and ring true (here Ramon parted company with the surrealists). But a fine gregueria rewards further reverie. In this example, if the river is a woman letting down her hair, then the waterfall becomes an erotic moment of surrender endlessly and deliciously prolonged.

• • •

When lemons rot they become sweet.

The uneaten becomes inedible, the unsaid unsayable.

Shallowness spreads.

A man builds his church on the ruins of his lust.

A miracle! But not the one I wanted.

Time will fix a bad haircut and kill the barber.

Mind is more kitchen than library.

I prefer books written at eye-level.

To worship is easier than to love.

A man's silence is medieval; a woman's baroque.

In youth I ordered a feast I've now no appetite for.

A man will give his whole life to pleasure but is ashamed to die for it.

If you've only a window-box, know every leaf.

Failure gives us our perimeters.

Any grail, long sought, becomes a holy grail.

The poorer I am, the more valuable my money.

Nature has laws but no lawyers.

Most leaves get rained on by other leaves.

Even 'too late' comes at its proper time.

Greguerias

Mop water is a rich consommé of footsteps.

This morning's donuts are now hard and cynical.

When drunk, I become a child's drawing of myself.

Dressed in moss pajamas, stone sleeps in the rain.

From salad to salad goes the handsome Prince of Pepper.

Each hammer blow is answered by a blow of silence.

Plates on a dish rack sleep standing up.

Loneliest of all is the bubble in a spirit level.

A stopped clock has arrived.

All skulls are laughing at the same joke.

A pillow turned cool side up has the coolness of turned earth.

The pathos of a dog is that its mouth is its hand.

Saddest of all? The parrot's uncomprehending face as it speaks.

Pajamas have a little pocket for the ticket stub from dreams.

The day moon is day-nurse of the insane.

The bottom half of a unicyclist is trying to escape.

Rust is the autumn of iron.

David Shields

The merit of style exists precisely in this: that it delivers the greatest number of ideas in the fewest number of words.[1]

How much can one remove and still have the composition be intelligible? This understanding, or its lack, divides those who can write from those who can really write. Chekhov removed the plot. Pinter, elaborating, removed the history, the narration; Beckett, the characterization. We hear it anyway. Omission is a form of creation.[2]

The Canterbury Tales, a compendium of all the good yarns Chaucer knew, has lasted centuries while the long-winded medieval narratives went into museums.[3]

As Stephen Frears, the director of *High Fidelity*, worked to translate the best moments of the Nick Hornby novel on which the movie was based, he found to his surprise that the best moments were the voiceovers, especially the direct speeches of Rob Gordon (John Cusack) to the camera. Frears said, "What we realized was that the novel

---

1 Victor Schlovsky, *Theory of Prose*.

2 David Mamet, "Hearing the Notes that Aren't Played," *The New York Times*.

3 Ezra Pound, *The ABC of Reading*.

was a machine to get to twelve crucial speeches in the book about romance and art and music and list-making and masculine distance and the masculine drive for art and the masculine difficulty with intimacy." This is the way I experience most novels: you have to read seven hundred pages to get the handful of insights that were the reason the book was written, and the apparatus of the novel is there as a huge, elaborate, overbuilt stage set.

"I'm a third of the way through Thomas Bernhard's *The Loser* and at first I was excited by it, but now I'm a little bored. I may not finish it."

"It's so beautiful and so pessimistic."

"Yes, but it doesn't hold one's interest the way a nineteenth-century novel does. I'm never bored when I'm reading George Eliot or Tolstoy."

"I am."

"And you're not bored when you're reading Bernhard?"

"I'm bored by plot. I'm bored when it's all written out, when there isn't any shorthand."[4]

Charles Darwin was known to slice a fat book in half – to make it easier to handle – or to rip out any sections he wasn't interested in.

The line of beauty is the line of perfect economy.[5] It is my ambition to say in ten sentences what everyone else says in a whole book – what everyone else does not say in a whole book.[6]

• • •

---

4 Janet Malcom, "Conversations with David Salle," in *Forty-One False Starts*.

5 Ralph Waldo Emerson, "*Beauty*."

6 Friedrich Nietzsche, *Twilight of the Idols*

Resolution and conclusion are inherent in a plot-driven narrative.

Story seems to say that everything happens for a reason, and I want to say, *No, it doesn't.*

If I'm reading a book and it seems truly interesting, I tend to start reading back to front in order not to be too deeply under the sway of progress.

The absence of plot leaves the reader room to think about other things.

With relatively few exceptions, the novel sacrifices too much, for me, on the altar of plot.

The novel is dead. Long live the antinovel, built from scraps.

I'm not interested in collage as the refuge of the compositionally disabled. I'm interested in collage as (to be honest) an evolution beyond narrative.

Everything I write, I believe instinctively, is to some extent collage. Meaning, ultimately, is a matter of adjacent data.

Momentum, in literary mosaic, derives not from narrative but from the subtle, progressive buildup of thematic resonances.

Thomas Jefferson went through the New Testament and removed all the miracles, leaving only the teachings. Take a source, extract what appeals to you, discard the rest. Such an act of editorship is bound to reflect something of the individual doing the editing: a plaster cast of an aesthetic – not the actual thing, but the imprint of it.

– the transformation, through framing, of outtakes into totems.

The problem of scale is interesting. How long will the reader stay engaged? I don't mean stay dutifully but stay charmed, seduced, and beguiled. Robbe-Grillet's *Ghosts in the Mirror*, which he calls a Romanesque, is a quasi-memoir with philosophical reflections, intimate flashes, and personal addresses to the reader. About this length, I think: 174 pages.

You don't need a story. The question is how long do you not need a story?

The gaps between paragraphs = the gaps between people (content tests form).

Nonfiction, qua label, is nothing more or less than a very flexible (easily breakable) frame that allows you to pull the thing away from narrative and toward contemplation, which is all I've ever wanted.

When plot shapes a narrative, it's like knitting a scarf. You have this long piece of string and many choices about how to knit, but we understand a sequence is involved, a beginning and an end, with one part of the weave very logically and sequentially connected to the text. You can figure out where the beginning is and where the last stitch is cast off. Webs look orderly too, but unless you watch the spider weaving, you'll never know where it started. It could be attached to branches or table legs or eaves in six or eight places. You won't know the sequence in which the different cells were spun and attached to one another. You have to decide for yourself how to read its patterning, but if you pluck it at any point, the entire web will vibrate.

Richard Kostelanetz

I've been trying to write aphorisms my entire literary life. The first inspiration was probably the Chinese fortune cookie, whose beginnings in America seem uncertain. For the university literary magazine, my first contribution as a freshman was wise-guy redefinitions of political terms, probably influenced by Max Nomad's *A Skeptics Political Dictionary.* I liked my own efforts enough to reprint much of them in my *Skeptical Essays*.

Many of the great American comedians are aphorists and the greatest was a woman, of course, Mae West.

Long interested in alternative forms for familiar things, in this case the succinct English sentence, I've been trying to write many of them within the limit of four words. I call them MINIMAXIMS. For others, my words form continuous circles lacking either beginning or end. These I call INFINITIES.

More sparely, I've tried INSTANCES, which have two or three words. I've even tried two kinds with only one word – MEDITATIONS (which subsume thoughts), and BULL'S EYES (which are perceptions). I've put these collections aside to focus more on the nexus of literature and book art. May I return to aphorisms soon.

• • •

To be happy, be.

Easier imagined than realized.

Those bloodless can't blush.

Favor ethics over esthetics.

Great jokes incorporate truths.

Narcissism is self-limiting.

Democracy depends upon meetings.

Numbers aren't people.

Heaven includes strangers, alas.

Never, ever, be redundant.

Aphorists repeat differently.

Cultural class is scarce.

Strong scissors cut thick.

Celebrity's a fool's desire.

Great imagination transcends evidence.

Self-indulgence depends upon self-confidence.

Evangelists frighten nearly everyone.

Came, saw, worried, failed.

Behind jargon is cowardice.

Success is luck repeated.

Trousers remake a woman.

Desire can't be faked.

One obsession cures another.

Self-analysis incorporates self-deception.

Racecar spells racecar backwards.

Everyone discriminates, even unconsciously.

Truest fantasies remain untested.

Money can purchase fame.

Insecurity generates more insecurity.

Drunks think they're smart.

Gabby people entertain themselves.

Be not earliest worm.

All secrets are temporary.

Beautiful people easily deceive.

Ann Lauinger

A phorism is the least approximate of genres, the opposite of a phlegmatic "Whatever…" Reading an aphorism is like getting right to the punch-line of a good joke without having to go through any of the preliminaries. In some quarters, the aphorism has a staid, even stolid, reputation as a perpetuator of changeless wisdom. But this is a very partial view, neglecting the form's potential for disruption, its underlying violence. An aphorism's packed and pointed zingy-ness is built to administer (deftly) a real jolt. When one of these rich little pinpoint explosions goes off, happy-making endorphins flood my brain. No wonder they're as addictive as pistachio nuts – just as delicious and easier to open.

But do aphorisms really have something to say, or are they all show? They've certainly been pressed into service by thinkers of all stripes, metaphysical, ethical, and scientific, from the pre-Socratics to Nietzsche. Francis Bacon thought the establishment of aphorisms a necessary step in the dismantling of false systems of thought and the growth of true knowledge. The aphorisms I enjoy unsettle as much as they nail down. Often they execute a small but devastating twist on a traditional saying, turning it inside out. The aphorism's compactness seems to attract paradox and oxymoron as moths to a flame – only their lightning sizzle and zap isn't gone in an instant; it's preserved, to be revisited whenever you crave that electric tingle.

Some aphorisms are butterflies: their beauty is immediately apprehensible, yet imply the genesis of an argument, a whole history of cocoon and caterpillar for the reader to mull over.

My favorite aphorisms are those which startle me into laughter first and then into thought.

• • •

As the crow flies, she simplifies.

The same line defines circle and cipher.

Seen from the labyrinth, a kite is not so lovely as its string.

All's fair and well that ends in love, not war.

A cat may look at a king, but why should it bother?

Vinaigrette and flattery both need a good dash of salt.

If you don't have anything nice to say, post a comment.

Allegory – in other words, other worlds.

Smoking provides a lot of pleasant times and then kills you – rather like life.

When the moon in the sea looked at the sky, she was enchanted with her reflection.

The emptier the vessel, the more it comprehends.

Music reminds me how little I know – and how little it matters.

No dog is a connoisseur of sunsets.

Distressed and clingy: perfect for blue jeans, lousy for lovers.

In Paradise there was no verb but *to be*.

Every frog croaks its own note, yet all jump in the pond with the same splash.

Anti-evolutionists may be their own best argument.

How dare we condescend to the Middle Ages? For their miracles and relics, ecstasies, and rituals we have our anti-oxidants and magnets, kidney cleansings and Fitbit.

The body is the new soul.

When even the truth comes in so many varieties –
plain, simple, whole, unvarnished – should we be
surprised by the proliferation of lies?

I, too, would burn my candle at both ends, if I could
find the right candleholder.

Holly Woodward

Someone who can write aphorisms shouldn't fritter his time away writing essays, Karl Kraus said.

The sentence is my favorite mind-altering substance.

Adults discouraged my efforts to talk. Thank you to all my teachers – and who isn't one?

I don't believe everything I say.

You open your heart and the world yawns back.

It is easier to tell the truth if no one believes you.

Sometimes you need to speak loudly to the universe, so you hear.

At first I told the truths that would hurt others. Then I told the truths that would hurt me most.

Writing is quiet frenzy.

Every afternoon, I reach the end of my rope, but like a spider I keep spinning the story line out of my body.

With age comes wisdom, and then she wanders off.

My cat lazes on my desk, tapping pens and paperweights until they fall over the edge. I do the same with the thoughts in my head.

• • •

I don't want to be forgiven. I want to be loved for my sins.

"I do not fantasize about love affairs that never happened,"
"Lied the novelist."

In my old age, I'm particular about whom I'll cry over.

If you're on a roll, you're probably headed downhill.

Love does not understand the word, "No." That's how you tell.

In writing, you have to reinvent the wheel over and over and then lash yourself to it.

I may be nobody, but nobody is me.

To live with someone who loves you is to become chatelaine of his imaginary castle. But the skeletons in the closet are real.

Mind is the way time holds itself together.

The first day of spring: Time to officially throw in the towel on last year's spring cleaning projects.

Avoid the plague like clichés.

My education was attempted taxidermy on me.

Nothing costs me as much as things I have stolen.
Hearts, for one.

The heart is a wound, the mind – a scar.

Want wants to know how. It is not interested in why.

Every star, every black hole, every flea, bug, beetle,
ocean, cloud, and wind is necessary for us to exist.
And all of it, every single thing we need, is dangerous.

The world is not black or white. It is flickering.

Eye candy causes mental cavities.

If you find the idea of hell for others a comfort, you are living in it now.

Metaphor comes from the Ancient Greek words 'to carry over.' Metaphor carries the unknown to the known. It also takes, like a riptide, the known and plunges it back into the unknown.

What kind of equation is love? One without an equal sign.

If your life is improbable, you can't write it as fiction.

Steven Carter

Years ago, my wife asked one of her second-graders, a math prodigy named Stephen, how he was able to do fairly complex equations at such a tender age.

The little guy responded aphoristically,

"I don't know. I just know that I know."

I always recall that anecdote when readers ask me where my aphorisms come from.

Answering far less profoundly than did Stephen, I say, "I don't know. I just know that I receive them."

Not very illuminating, I realize, but it's the truth. Like poetry – and the best aphorisms out there *are* poetry, in my estimation – if they don't come through you like a dose of salts, they'd better not come through at all.

Jack Spicer, after the death of Wallace Stevens the American poet that I most admire, had something like this in mind when he gave a series of lectures at the 1965 Vancouver Poetry Festival. Like William Blake and W.B. Yeats before him, Spicer believed in what he called "poetry by dictation," a process that goes against the grain of what the poet *wants* to say:

I think [an important] step for the poet of dictation is when he finds out that [a good poem] says exactly the opposite of what he wants to say... Like if you want to say something about your beloved's eyebrows and the poem says the eyes should fall out, and you don't really want the eyes to fall out; or you're trying to write a poem on Vietnam and you write a poem about ice-skating in Vermont...

For me, doing aphorisms is something like that. It's as if the muse is telling you, "Talk all you want, Baby, but *then* let's go to bed," meaning that you can try your hardest to pack something brilliant into one or two or three lines, but in the end, you have to give the aphorism (or the parable and fable, which I've happened onto very recently) free rein.

One might also say "free reign," since it's been made quite clear to me, in the six years or so that I've been writing aphorisms, who's really running the show. And it ain't me.

• • •

The wish to soar on wings of the imagination *is* wings of the imagination. Too easy, you say. But how many of us wish to soar on wings of the imagination?

Yes, we are possessed by the devil because we are lonely and he is lonely; but in which order?

In the prison of our bodies we dread the moment when the cell door is flung open.

What in the world possesses the devil?

Fool me once, shame on you; fool me twice, shame on you; always shame on you.

Much can be tolerated by condemning it.

Something in us enjoys bringing bad news, even when it concerns ourselves.

Believing that the bell tolls for you is like believing that the barmaid means it when she calls you "darlin'."

This morning: the unquenchable grieving of the sound of rain. We are the cup it drinks from.

Peace of soul is denied to us, not because we lead troubled lives, but because we don't.

The best remedy for worry is disaster.

Christianity – a religion of substitutions: grape juice for wine; wine for blood; wafer for flesh; priest or pastor for saint; prayer for penitence.

For primitive man: stars and stones, period.
No substitutions, please!

Last dreary reminder of the imperfection of Man: *I can make fun of myself, but you can't make fun of me.*

To me the greatest argument against the existence of a divine intelligence isn't suffering but mediocrity.

Parables

Kafka writes, "Leopards break into the temple and drink to the dregs what is in the sacrificial pitchers; this is repeated over and over again; finally it can be calculated in advance, and it becomes part of the ceremony."

Let us go further. After an even longer time, the temple congregation begins to worship the leopards as gods, until one man rises and says in a loud voice, "I can remember how you broke in here in the old days; you are merely intruders, false gods!" The congregation grows restless and begins whispering.

Then the leopards reply, "But we are not false gods. We are leopards."

The congregation resumes its worship.

On the day that animals acquired the power of speech, we were astounded to discover that they had nothing interesting to say!

Nevertheless, we lay awake at night, restless, troubled, straining to hear them whispering about us.

In the Kingdom of the Lizard and the Dragon, King Lizard and King Dragon meet occasionally and perform a strange ritual.

King Lizard says to King Dragon, "You are too big to eat. Therefore you are nobody to me."

King Dragon says to King Lizard, "You are too little to eat. Therefore *you* are nobody to me."

King Lizard and King Dragon return amicably to their palaces.

So long as King Lizard and King Dragon agree that each is nobody to the other, peace and harmony reign in the Kingdom of the Lizard and the Dragon.

The people of a village heard a church bell ringing somewhere in the distance, but where? It couldn't have come from the village church, for they heard the mysterious bell on every day but Sunday, the only day when the village church bell was not stilled.

They flocked into the countryside, each in search of the mysterious bell. Some heard it here, some heard it there, but the bell was never found.

Soon each wandering villager fell down on his knees and worshipped the point in the air where he heard the mysterious bell. And the village church was deserted and its bell silenced forever, for the villagers rested on the seventh day.

What would wisdom seem like in a parallel universe where plus is minus and black is white? Not as different as you and I might think!

Two women were brought before King Solomon; both lay claim to the same child; each argued eloquently on her own behalf. Solomon listened patiently, then dismissed them, saying that they would have his decision the next day.

The next day both women appeared, beaming in anticipation of Solomon's judgment. He said, "It is my decree that both of you shall be cut in half to make one woman, so that the child may have its proper mother."

Two identical bald men sit down at table. Pointing to his bald pate, one says, "On *me* it looks good." The other agrees, "On *you* it looks good." Both are comforted.

George Murray

My introduction to writing aphorisms came through James Richardson. I had been invited to give a talk about Canadian poetry at Princeton, and the organizers paired me with James to read from my fourth book – sonnets – at a lovely church. James read from *Vectors* and I was deeply impressed. As we had a bite to eat after, we discussed the form and James mentioned that many of the closing couplets from my book would make ideal aphorisms if removed whole from their host poems. He suggested that I probably had a few more aphorisms hiding in the pages of my journals, and that I should go through them to check. When I returned to Canada I found I had not only a few, but nearly 1000 over five years of journals. They were like little nuggets of poetry that had never become poems, I thought. But that wasn't even true: the best of them were much more than nuggets. They were whole units that required no "poem" around them to be fully realized. They were finished; little inky arts hiding among the failed scribbles in the white. This was an awakening for me.

I was enchanted by the form from the beginning, but never more than when arranging the collected aphorisms into a full book. *Glimpse* has 409 aphorisms arranged five to a page, in a sort of sine wave of thought, where each subtly leads into the next, each group of five bound by theme over the course of the book. This creates a situation in which the aphorisms are constantly loaning (and borrowing from) each other a weight and momentum that makes a sum greater than its parts. I began this structure as a way to help myself get through the book-building process, but in the end it became an integral part of how I look at the art of building and arranging the aphorism for public consumption.

When I talk about aphorisms to those not familiar with the form, I describe them as poems without all the poetry getting in the way. But, for all I know, philosophers might describe them as thoughts without all the philosophy getting in the way. Aphorisms occupy a borderland between poetry and philosophy, a space that is not quite either, but shares elements of both. They combine philosophy's heavy work of deep thought with poetry's elegance and surprise of the well-expressed. The best of them feel almost like pieces of folk wisdom you haven't yet heard. I know I've hit one right on when the piece strikes me as something new or true in its ideas, but familiar and worn in its delivery. Almost like the pleasure we get from hearing proverbs. When I write an aphorism and think, *Surely it's been said like this before, surely it's a piece of common wisdom*, that's when I know I have it right. That's when it gives me shivers.

• • •

As with the knife, the longer the conversation, the less frequently it comes to a point.

Knowledge is what happens when you rob suspicion of doubt.

Rubble becomes ruin when the tourists arrive.

The one-legged bird is not so bad off.

To those who wonder whether the strangers we see in our dreams are actually other dreamers, I say, it is more urgent to wonder whether the strangers we see in our waking hours are actually other people.

Panic is worry on a tight schedule.

Beauty is found with a quick glance; the grotesque is found by close study.

Anyone who yells loud enough can be famous among the pigeons.

Routine breeds sameness, shields mediocrity, and creates happiness.

Standards fall like pants: easily and on their own, once past a certain point.

Is chance that which we *didn't* expect or that which we *couldn't* expect?

The universe remains mum on the subject of itself, yet still we hold the mic to its lips as though waiting for comment.

When strangers acknowledge one another it is always in the brotherhood of condition.

The first level of charity is imagining the needy.

The good news is: you're loved. The bad news is: so are your enemies.

Turning forty is like looking up and realizing it's two in the afternoon.

You can judge entire societies by the expressions on the faces of their dolls.

Suspicion and evidence are always holding the elbows of intuition.

Models have that vacant look because they aren't allowed to stare back.

Harmony is coincidence harnessed.

Myth is just how consciousness handles instinct.

Just like the scar hidden beneath the hairline, so too do all predilections become apparent with age.

Falling asleep is not like falling down stairs; it's like falling up them.

The coffin's satin is life's pink slip.

In the city and the woods both, the scent of fire causes panic, but by the lake it only causes guitars.

Both is the choice of kings.

You holiday with death for a while, then it's back to work.

Urgency is a product of pessimism.

Resolve to always be the last one clapping as the applause dies, and someday you'll also be the first as it begins.

Forgetting what happened is also a part of what happened.

In martyrs and poets both, the rumour of greatness is enough to stave off criticism.

It's not that there's nothing to regret, but that I've narrowed down what I can regret simply by having shown up.

Charity is what we give to make things go away.

The universe is a table too wide to have corners.

Everyone works in sales now.

Justice is never black and white, except on cop cars and killer whales.

Sleep is the rough draft of death.

Until you've seen some sign of your prey, you're not hunting, you're walking.

Writing the erotic poem is like ironing in the nude – sexy for women, dangerous for men.

We're already being studied by the future.

The prime struggle: finding out how to spend your time instead of having it spent for you.

Truth is whatever piece of information would have been useful to have before the conversation began.

It's not in my heart to commit murder, though it may very well be in my hands.

It's not easy to be me, but I know that's true for you, too.

Manners are inherited answers to inherited problems.

Revelers feel insulted by one who doesn't join them, even if he wasn't invited.

The only bad thing about luck is that we don't get to choose how it's applied.

Even fully dressed, some people wear nothing but the fingerprints of others.

The slot machine is the idiot's ATM.

Getting old doesn't bother me, but staying old does.

The trees on the edge of the forest are the ones with the most leaves.

Alex Stein

I came to the aphorism by way of haiku and I came to haiku by ways still vague to me. I was 25, living in Seattle, and in thrall to the prose of Jack Kerouac. I spent my days and evenings filling notebook after notebook with stream of consciousness twaddle.

Perhaps, I would have continued at this until I was good and dead. There was really no reason not to. I enjoyed the activity. Notebooks were cheap. The hours flew by.

Then something odd: in the middle of the twaddle, I wrote a little poem.

Dandelion, roar!
Simple thing,
speak your simple mind.

I looked at the poem, and here is the curious thing: the poem looked back at me.

Not long after that I wrote:

Hold light,
butterfly;
for a short life:
Praise!

The more I looked at these poems, the more they looked back at me. "What?" I asked. "What do you want?" "Divine us," they replied. "How?" I asked. "Divine us," they repeated.

In a bookstore on Capitol Hill, I found a haiku anthology. In it, I read Kikaku's:

Above the boat,
bellies
of wild geese.

Over the next few years, I must have read that poem a thousand times. Then, one day, I wrote in the margin:

Perhaps our world is the spirit world of some other world. Perhaps our birdsongs are heard but faintly in some other world, and only by certain ears. Perhaps a poem is like an airlock that carries the breath of one world into the lungs of the next.

I read Kikaku's:

Evening bridge,
a thousand hands
cool on the rail.

I wrote:

Kikaku's bridge spans both the construct of space and the abstract of time; so, all those hands, "cool on the rail," are also the hands of the dead in their various phases of crossing-over.

Kikaku! That was the unlikely name of the piper who led me on.

• • •

In the whorl of our fingerprints there is something of the original design that lingers, and in the palms of our hands some residue of those ancient rivers that bore us here. It is just as the poet Blake suggested: The joys of the body are the joys of the angels; the sorrows of the imagination are the sorrows of the world.

Editor to poet says: "Either poetry holds a charge or it does not hold a charge. Your poetry holds a charge. I would only be the mad electrician who strips away the insulation to make the lines more dangerous."

Grace cannot be won, sanity cannot be bestowed. Since you cannot fight for your Grace, fight for your sanity. And your Grace, should it come, may find you ready.

"How are your boundaries holding up?" he asks her with a devilish grin. "Terribly well, I'm afraid," she replies, lying as one does to the devil not so much to maintain one's virtue as to maintain one's self-respect.

In one sense the cosmos is a puzzle box that can be unlocked and is full of secret drawers and compartments, but in another sense there is no puzzle box and all the secrets are our own.

Poetry (all thought, really) is the ripple from a stone that has broken the surface of a still water.

There are gems of art hidden in plain sight everywhere. The frost on a winter window pane is a masterpiece of abstract expression.

The life flowing into the writing and out again must be as the sleeping mind is to the mind awake: both a resource and a thing unto itself.

Your symbols are not my symbols but symbols are all
we have and no symbol is enchanted but meaning is.

Fire, from birth, reaches
toward fire; and water,
seeking water, will carve its way
underground, if it must,
to achieve (re)union.

To analyze the life of an artist through his work is
like analyzing personality via dream interpretation.
One can find correlations, but there is always the
possibility that a dream is not a mirror, but another
world entirely.

Academia is a jungle in which one must not devour
without seeming first to pause.

Scribble, scribble, erase;
Scribble, erase, scribble
Scribble, scribble, scribble.
Erase, erase, erase.

There are two directions toward which any of us can aspire: greatness of the personality or greatness of the humanity. And these two directions are mutually exclusive. The former depends upon amplification. The latter upon surrender.

One law of Karma: Whatever you mock you will eventually become. That is why I mock only the rich and the beautiful.

Theory is the ghost that rises from the corpse upon the dissecting table.

Nabokov said "reality" is the only word in the English language that should always be surrounded by quotation marks. Not "reality" but "dream."

Two people are arguing over an empty box: their struggle is its only content.

If anyone ever asked me what I would exchange for charisma – and I mean real charisma, rock and roll charisma – I would tell them "my common sense," because anyhow that seems to be the standard bargain.

The continual struggle of the artist to become invisible in the art – as the soul is invisible in the man.

An artist died and went to heaven where he was greeted by an archangel who said, "Welcome! I suppose you have many questions." "What?" cried the artist, "was my art not good enough to get me damned?"

The Self, the real Self, is buried so deeply (hear its muffled cries?) that to make its re-acquaintance is death's (and sex's) true lure.

Where we are, there our grace may begin.

Each of us has, deep within, the seed of something that, without malice, seeks our annihilation. (As, one might say more cheerfully, winter has summer.)

The archetypal, from which the deepest poems are drawn, is an ancient machine that the gods left behind when they went off to found their next universe.

Fill your joy cup, while the fountain is at hand.

Hart Pomerantz

I love the twists of logic in jokes. This penchant started me writing aphorisms. As a kid I loved comedy, and particularly *non-sequiturs*. My mother used to say to me, "Hart, take off your sweater, I'm hot." She was serious but I thought it was funny.

My interest in comedy eventually led me to Hollywood as a comedy writer for the hit show "Laugh-In." Later, I was fortunate enough to have a writing session with Woody Allen, the greatest joke writer of them all. From these experiences as well as from being a full-time lawyer, I developed a love of word play, the 'sleight of mouth,' the witty remark. Getting laughs that included a philosophic insight seemed even more desirable. For me an aphorism is a joke that went to college.

When I write these one-liners, they seem to pop out without thought. It is impossible for me to know what is going to appear on the page until I read it. It amazes me that the same brain can write drivel one moment and the next moment produce a diamond.

• • •

Law school taught me how to take two situations that are exactly the same and show how they are different.

Let all the gods fight it out, and we'll worship the winner.

Man's need for answers far outweighs his need for truth.

A president near the end of his second term resembles an old stripper who has removed all her clothes yet still has twenty minutes left in her act.

In a perfect world the woman would also fall asleep after sex.

The tip of the iceberg is all that is left.

When driving south we are passing through the future of those driving north.

Never trust a country whose army marches without bending its knees.

Hero worship requires no clergy.

A dictator lives in fear because he knows there are others out there just like him.

Why is absolute power so bad, and Absolut vodka so good?

Prison separates the guilty members of society from those not yet apprehended.

We must stop describing what we cannot see.

The righteous often become the trophies of the mighty.

In the beginning there was nothing. In the end there was Wal-Mart.

The less the difference between people the greater the animosity.

The rug must be held responsible for its fringe.

It is unfortunate that no school teaches us how to fail properly.

The nuclear family has been detonated.

Should you be considered an original thinker if you discover a new method of stealing ideas?

A boy born with a silver spoon in his mouth soon discovers how easily it can progress up to his nose.

In prehistoric times whenever there was thunder, religion soon followed.

He was a type A minus personality.

All professions invent their own jargon in order to charge you for the translation.

Do lobsters ever feel they're being rescued when the waiter reaches into the tank?

James Guida

For me, the interest in aphorisms began back in university, as part of the reading I was doing alongside my studies, maybe at the expense of them. I'd chanced upon a copy of La Rochfoucauld's *Maxims* in a Melbourne bookstore. Leafing through it at home, I was struck by the work's lucid and surgical brilliance, and wondered how I'd never heard of it. My age or experience meant that certain lines went over my head, and even the ones I laughed at sometimes needed puzzling out first. It was a bit unreal: to think that such force could exist in that few words. I eventually got into Chamfort, Valéry, Lao-Tzu, Cioran and other people, and would hunt down any and every lead. Different kinds of reading were absorbing me too, but with aphorisms there was a special hunger. I think in some ways the form, and in particular its often mordant style of humor, answered my situation at the time. There was more to it, of course: it was also about trying to see freshly, to test all your assumptions and ideas. Were people allowed to say these things, how did they come to think of them? Which thoughts were true, and if they were, how?

At some point I started trying to write the aphorisms I would have been pleased to encounter and felt were missing, as though all aphorisms comprised a single big, but not big enough collection. I had little to say, and what did emerge sometimes looked baffling later. (In a youthful letter, Swift curses his efforts to make even an old shoe come out intelligibly on the page. A shoe! I would have been content with that.) Still, the practice seemed good for someone wanting to learn how to write – from the ground up. I kept at it and came to value how the pursuit worked as a means of clarifying and speculating about various themes, some of them personal. For a long time I had no thoughts of trying to publish, or so I tell myself, since apparently at a party once I reported that I was working on a book. Could both accounts be right? Perhaps intentions are beside the point. My impression is that aphorisms are as much about the unwritten, the unwilled as they are about writing, and that the form's best discoveries tend to appear plucked from a space outside the individual's frame.

• • •

Not to count chickens before they're hatched, eggs before they're laid, chickens who might possibly lay eggs, birds who from afar might be confused with chickens. Not to count or think of chickens.

A man sometimes seems annoyed when another man sits down beside him on the train. The thought seems to be: "I was saving that for an unknown beautiful woman!"

Awkwardness is collaborative.

For one person to accept advice from another, I mean to really take it on board, is as special and precise a phenomenon as the pollination of some fickle plant. The weather must be just so. Certain other plants will have an accidental role, and factors as small as insects' feet will come into play. The substance of the advice itself may well be secondary.

Sending an email can be like letting go of an animal.

The belief that you have no illusions – least attractive, least fruitful of illusions?

There is after all a criminal aspect to Solitude. It too would like to snuff out the witnesses.

Not answering, answering more slowly, answering with less. Today half the art of correspondence is in that.

Nothing less interesting than the conversation meant to be overheard.

There are no edges or grooves on the man's face, nothing at all on which to hook a gaze.

Basically, the whole affair threatened to make adults of us all.

Is it that we just want desires themselves, more than to have them gratified? I believe we do want satisfaction, plus renewal of desire, plus myriad unexpected good tidings.

Perfectly good fruit, simply in being bumped about by chance, indifferently sniffed at, idly handled and overlooked, is sometimes gradually made unfit for those who would otherwise choose it. So it is with lovers.

Bosses, like cats, should have to wear little bells to warn of their approach.

Critics of text-messaging are wrong to think it's a regressive form of communication. It demands so much concision, subtlety, psychological art – in fact, it's more like pulling puppet strings than writing.

I don't want to romanticize melancholy either ... Still, how princely is the white lobster at the New England Aquarium!

To give space to a pedestrian ahead, he slowed down so much that he was eventually going backward. Traveling backward, it became necessary to perform the same operation on the people heading the other way.

There are sentences so triumphant we imagine
we can make out the author in them, waving to us
delightedly from a float within the paragraph.

The notion of "sex objects" – where has it gone?
We're all sex or lust objects now, willingly, happily.
Anything to distract from our status as work objects, I
suppose.

Irreverence alone isn't enough, or else the word's
rhetorical. The best humor reveres joy.

Lily Akerman

When I'm in the mind to think of aphorisms – the writing of them is mostly thinking of them – I feel alert as a Geiger counter. I listen for the inaudible noise around me, the hidden paradoxes. I interrogate my own assumptions for ways in which I contradict myself. Do I really not know? Or am I afraid of what I do know? In conversation, I verge on being laconic (I'm listening), or a contrarian (I'm not, I'm being precise), or "intense" (but seriously, what is love?).

As a puppeteer might discover a jaw in a pair of scissors, I look for the latent life around me. Underneath any rock could lie an ecosystem. From one angle, the rock might resemble sadness, from another silence. The word Silence could be the subject of a whole dictionary.

I consider thoughts as surfaces. I zoom in like a micro-engraver and I zoom out like an astrophysicist.

I recently saw a microengraving by the artist Chen Zhong-Sen, who writes on surfaces smaller than a grain of rice. He carved a poem along a strand of hair. His work struck me as aphoristic, because like an aphorism, the form is born of intense concentration. When an aphorism is described as "sharp," maybe this is what we mean: it has a high concentration, of thought and language.

132

• • •

An aphorism is a little bang that implies a vast universe.

The first kiss in the world was a bite.

Predators are also prey.

Two drops merge when they touch. We don't. We are two cups, filled to the brim.

To wait, endure time. To be patient, forget it.

A puddle contains the sky.

It's all an illusion! you cry, as if the illusion were the lie.

If I could have two things, I'd wish first for imagination, then for desire. And with them would come hope.

In the heat of the moment, lukewarm feels cold.

I hold no grudge. The grudge follows me around.

Loving one who won't requite: scratch the bite, and scratch the bite.

Your flaws forgive mine.

The man who consults every opinion must then decide which opinion to believe.

It's not a dream until I wake.

Beggars can be choosers if they dare.

Always the same old argument. To resolve it would be devastating.

A sigh is a sunken wish.

It stings to clean a wound.

Who worries that he will have regrets will regret having worried.

The dance is not in the steps but in the impulses.

Reason is emotion in a suit.

It's the thought that counts, and the thought that must be held accountable.

The puppet cannot see its strings.

No harm in insulting the egotist. He will not know of whom you speak.

Self-deprecation is another kind of self-absorption.

Holding your breath won't save it.

A shadow's shadow's a man.

Decisions: little murders that keep us alive.

In the crevices of any routine lies improvisation.

The road, a bridge between bridges.

If only-ness, then loneliness.

Love's beginning and love's end are as unalike as diving and swimming.

The early bird gets the worm. The early worm dies.

Pessimists are optimists who hate to be disappointed.

Lose face, and what you will lose is a mask.

Thieves thieve. Thieves of thieves retrieve.

At the end of a great trial, the jury passes judgment. At the end of a great play, judgment cannot land.

Agreeing with critical thinkers does not mean you are one.

In some fears, I take comfort – if the spider went, I'd have to deal with the flies.

Charles Bernstein

Language is an event of the world, just as, for language users, the world is an event of language. Even the world is a word.

The work of art always exceeds its material embodiment. Physical or digital instantiations, anterior codes or algorithms, experience while reading or viewing, interpretations, contexts of publication or appearance, historical connections – all these have an affinity, clustering around an empty center.

In serial essay form, each of the interchanging parts relates tangentially to the next, forming a cluster around an unstated motif. In this way, different aspects of the imaginary are addressed, as if they were interlocking faces on the surface of a crystal.

Three types of fragmentation, or three aspects of any fragment: disjunction, ellipsis, constellation.

Serial frames, each displacing but not replacing one another.

Juxtaposing disparate, if related, material, forms a constellation within an environment.

". . . we attain to but brief and indeterminate glimpses." –[E. A. POE, *THE POETIC PRINCIPLE*]

• • •

I love originality so much I keep copying it.

Immature poets borrow. Mature poets invest.

Religion is giving religion a bad name.

Nor am I an atheist. I believe in the fallible gods of thought and in my resistance to these gods. I have faith in my aversion of faith.

I'm an observant Jew. I look closely at the things around me, as if they were foreign.

In the world of the imagination, impossible just means the next opportunity to get real.

Rather than an expression of love, justice is a protection against our inability to love.

We are most familiar with our estrangement; it is our home ground.

The absence of an accent is also an accent.

All the signs say no passage; still, there must be a way.

Show me a man with two feet firmly planted on the ground and I'll show you a man who can't get his pants on.

The rich do live better and have the narcotic of money to help them forget how it was acquired.

Be thorough: leave no turn unstoned.

To each his tone.

Thought is more resourceful than reality; that is why reality repudiates thought.

Everything is relative and if not relative it ought to be.

Let's just say that one day is completely different than the next, but they still connect and we call the pattern our lives.

Or how about: The storage you rent is equal to the mortgage you forgo.

Just because you think you can't change the world is not a reason to try any less.

Your desire for independence will ultimately be your slavery.

A bird calls but I hear only its song.

Existence needs essence the way a walking tour needs local color.

But a hole in an argument is not the same as a point of light.

The pen is tinier than the sword.

I'll give you a hand but only one.

That still, small voice may not be the root of all evil but it's no innocent bystander either.

The pit of the cherry is like the soul of a self-righteous man: when you find it, you want to spit it out.

"The world is everything that is the case." But the case is locked in the trunk of a stolen car.

Everything that happens is lost. Even what is recalled is lost in the recalling. Nonetheless, things go on happening.

My cares turned to wares.

I've got my next few years of work mapped out for me: figuring out what to do over the next few years.

Hue is a property of optics not objects.

You never know what invention will look like or else it wouldn't be invention.

So much depends upon what you are expecting.

The haze doesn't obscure the view it makes it palpable.

Memory is to life like a band-aid to a wound.

Making another patch for the patch.

It is equally problematic to shout "Theater!" at a crowded fire.

The arrival of a station at the train.

The questioning of the beautiful is always at least as important as the establishment of the beautiful.

Clinging to the loss as if it would protect you against the loss.

This is not a sentence.

Longing for nothing is often the only way to get anywhere.

Don't confuse the puzzle for the solution, the poet for the poem.

Save the last chance for me.

What's missing from the bird's eye view is plain to see on the ground.

In the 1990s, it was common in Russia to find stores with empty shelves, but one was stripped to bare walls. It was a shelf store.

Good poets make analogies, great poets make analogies between analogies.

I may be wrong, in fact I most surely am wrong, just not as wrong as you.

Olivia Dresher

The poetry I was reading and writing in the 1970s was usually short. Long poems generally lost me unless they contained aphoristic lines. I began keeping quotebooks of those lines. Reading poems and novels became a search for aphorisms embedded within the writing – aphorisms and fragments that were not only poetic but philosophical. I also began to write poems that contained aphoristic lines or titles.

My personal journals and notebooks became more fragmented and aphoristic. More and more they reflected the way I spontaneously thought and perceived. The poems I published were often "lifted" from my journals and shaped into traditional poetic form. But I began to feel that I'd rather write and publish fragments and aphorisms, not conventional poetry.

By the 1980s I began to speak of my journals and notebooks as the drafts of my main work. My collection of published diaries, journals, and notebooks continued to grow. I continued to "lift" poems from my notebooks and put them in non-notebook form, but I began to resist the process.

By the late 1980s/early 1990s my focus had changed to actively considering my journals and notebooks to be art forms in themselves. I also co-edited an anthology of contemporary journals, diaries, and notebooks – private writing as art. And I was discovering, reading, and collecting many published books of fragments and aphorisms.

"*That's* what I want to read, *that's* what I want to write," I could have said the first time I experienced a book of aphorisms. But I was too stunned to say anything. Aphorisms, at first, silenced me. I didn't know, yet, the freedom that short forms could inspire ... the *bravery* they could inspire. The way brevity and wordplay combine to create waves of possibilities. The way experimenting with words and ideas within a small framework feels expansive. The way the formlessness of the form triggers insights that seem to come out of nowhere. The way *Write that down, right now!* would become an almost daily chant.

• • •

Life is a mask hiding death, death is a mask hiding life.

To speak a cliché is to scratch an itch.

A bed is a torture chamber to an insomniac.

The older you get, the more everything is over before it begins.

If I can't fly, then let me fall as freely as rain.

Jokes are never lies, except those that aren't funny.

The closest thing to heaven is a beautiful graveyard.

They smile in photos like they dye their hair – to cover the gray.

The world is on fire, but they walk around with their coats on.

Nothing lasts these days except what we throw away.

They say: don't take it personally if someone doesn't love you. I say: should I also not take it personally if someone *does*?

In person we're only puppets of ourselves.

Tenderness is humility.

Ordinary life is like a bad novel: clichés everywhere, and no real character development.

Proof that I've never grown up: all the questions I ask.

A lifetime is just one long Now.

What are my fragments? Parachutes that open as I fall through the night.

Irena Karafilly

Poppy (Penelope) Litwin was never meant to be more than a fictional character – a bright, feisty travel journalist with a penchant for scribbling bon mots in her journal. When Yugoslavia fell apart, she wrote: "The only country in the world where there are more than two sides to the story, all incredible." When her husband betrayed her, she wrote: "Falling out of love is like falling anywhere: you pick yourself up, brush yourself off, and keep on going, hoping no one saw you." She was certainly an exceptional woman, but her most unexpected achievement was to turn her bemused creator into a budding aphorist. Poppy's own story eventually came to an end, but her epigrammatic propensities had somehow penetrated the interstices of my own brain, never to be expunged.

In retrospect, this surprises me less than it did at the time. I had, it seems, quite simply been an aphorist manqué. Although I had already published fiction, non-fiction, and poetry, it had never occurred to me to record my philosophical musings, let alone ponder the makings of an aphorist. But once I became one, I did start to wonder.

Writing aphorisms requires, I think, a keen eye, a certain analytical detachment, an obsession with words, an appreciation of pithy insights. Subjected to close scrutiny, aphorisms often beg to be challenged, but this may well be part of their charm; if they are not necessarily true, they are often deliciously provocative or witty.

But an aphorist, unlike the party wit, is not really out to entertain. We are delighted to elicit appreciative chuckles, but most of us are, I think, thwarted philosophers rather than court jesters. Many among us are avowed misanthropes, but a misanthrope, to my mind, is merely an idealist with a broken heart. The more grandiloquent in our midst may tell you that we are forever in search of Eternal Truths. And if these prove eternally elusive – well, at least there is the consolation of an elegantly stated apercu. There may be some arrogance in making sweeping pronouncements about the human condition, but surely age must confer a few entitlements to offset the discomfort of an increasingly jaundiced eye. Wisdom, as my own estimable heroine stated, is a consolation prize one accepts with a toothless smile.

Oh, and one more thing: Should you contemplate inviting one of us to a dinner party, you might be disappointed to find we are not all Oscar Wildes or George Bernard Shaws. Some of us indeed can be surprisingly tongue-tied on the social stage. But give us a piece of paper – a restaurant napkin or cigarette box will do – and, sooner or later, we'll retreat to the vast sea of our personal experience, combing its shores for some subtly-hued pebble, to be polished with a maddened sage's spit, a gleeful aesthete's devotion. It can be made to shine like a pearl but, expertly aimed, could sometimes prove fatal.

• • •

A good-will divorce is like having all your teeth extracted and having to smile.

The really amazing thing about history is not that it so often repeats itself, but that it fails to bore us.

The only power you have over other people is the ability to do without them.

Early recognition spoils some writers but posthumous recognition saves none.

People are at their most brilliant while defending themselves against their own conscience.

There are people who would give up custody of their children but fight over a first edition.

Astrology is the one religion with practically no believers and countless followers.

A critic may have to praise a friend's book, but he shouldn't be expected to read it too.

As an investment in the future, there is nothing more risky than parenthood.

Politicians are people who raised a hand at school but then forgot what they meant to say.

Law and justice are a horse and mule harnessed to the same cart, pulling in opposite directions.

People plan elaborate weddings to make a change of heart all but impossible.

Impossible not to wonder what Hitler's mother listened to while she was pregnant.

It's hardest of all to forgive those whom we have disappointed.

Allying yourself with the Left or the Right guarantees one outcome: you're left without the right to think for yourself.

Christopher Cokinos

The morning began with a maxim from Oprah Winfrey on the side of a coffee cup from Starbucks: "Know what sparks the light in you. Then use that light to illuminate the world." The day ended with a chance encounter with a series of surrealist proverbs by Paul Eluard and Benjamin Peret, including this one: "Cold meat lights no fire." I don't expect that on my latte any time soon. We seem to want memorable sentences as much as we want stories, and those sentences, like stories, can be set into the two great categories of the human condition: As It Should Be and As It Is. In the former, we can place maxims and proverbs like Winfrey's, sentences meant for guidance and comfort.

The aphorism, in contrast, directs us – more directly or rather indirectly – to the As It Is, as, famously, from Heraclitus: "One does not step into the same river twice." This is not a moral proposition or dictate; it is a literal and metaphoric fact. Perhaps the aphorism, like a poem, tends to do more than one thing at once, while a maxim or proverb is rooted to a single meaning.

I read for feeling, for tone, for facts, for a lovely sentence or two. I prefer atmosphere over plot. Thirty years ago, I chanced on Guy Davenport's translations of Heraclitus and Diogenes. I fell in love with maxims and

aphorisms – and with ancient fragments – right then. I
began taping index cards over my tiny college desk with
quotes from "Chariots of Fire" and Homer. I was trying to
find strategies for living.

Now, lately, I've been reading about the neuroscience
of affirmations – laying down new neural pathways by
repeating uplifting phrases. So we're back to Oprah
Winfrey, but that's okay.

I'd also like to think that enigmatic aphorisms – here's
one: "Cherries fall when texts fail" – lay down new neural
networks as compelling as the happy highways of self-help
synapses, because the odd never gets old.

• • •

Time is the deepest wilderness in which we wander.

How many species of disappointment in your field
guide?

Sun lights the top of cedars: I will rest my chin in my
hand for another hour.

Just sex? Just oxygen?

We each have beginner's mind, beginner's skin.

One stroke where one will do.

The moan, a hymn.

A chair in grass. Dew & Shadow. Still seeking God?

Sunset lights a cup, a blade, a wheel.

Work with your back to the clock.

It's not enough to close your windows against the wind.

Cries are clearer when the air is still.

A guest in a house should not remove its walls.

Willow leaves have cast shadows for fifty million years.

Even weeds sup water.

A full moon is only half.

Michael Theune

My search for metaphysical Truth probably went on somewhat longer than is seemly: not only did I study English and philosophy as an undergraduate, but, having received a scholarship, I went on to study philosophy and theology for two years at Oxford. My protracted search for cosmic certainty can perhaps be forgiven if one allows that for a minister's kid, which I am, the spiritual life can have considerable weight and reality.

The result of my own extended engagement with philosophical and theological tradition was that the idea of Truth dissolved. This event was not as traumatic for me as it has been for others because as Truth disintegrated, truths emerged. The disappearance of my metaphysical certainty did not leave me bereft; rather, it reverted to a passion for striking language, for poetry and aphorisms.

I had long been interested in and amazed by powerful acts of language. Much of this intrigue stemmed from my religious upbringing: I was surrounded by proverbs, maxims, parables, gnomic wisdom. Some of it also was derived from my Midwestern childhood: I had been surrounded by homespun wisdom, cross-stitched sayings and platitudes, each day accompanied by a thought-for-the-day.

The passion was kept alive during my investigation into philosophy and theology. My reading list consisted not only of works involving systems and theories, but the work of thinkers, including Pascal, Nietzsche, and Wittgenstein, whose works inspire wonder at the power of language.

So, even as systems gave way, my intellect, my imagination, and even my ear were being offered a new kind of life, the sparks and explosions of transformation. I was not sure a system could be derived from them, but that barely mattered: the moments were valuable in and of themselves. They were worth discovering, and I sought them out, whether by mystics or heretics, skeptics or saints. I discovered the work of Novalis and Elias Canetti's *The Agony of Flies*, Dag Hammarskjöld's *Markings* and Theodor Adorno's *Minima Moralia*, Jean Baudrillard's *Fragments* and Simon Weil's *Gravity and Grace*.

My most significant discovery, however, was the work of E.M. Cioran. The dark romance of Cioran's later aphorisms, their passionate pessimism, offered a kind of antidote for me: it leant music and intrigue to a skeptical worldview, suggesting that it too had its own exquisite poetry. As my own conclusions collapsed, I was enchanted by such elegant bewilderment, by the Ciorin's ability to articulate sighs.

It was Canetti, however, who wrote:

In growing, knowledge changes shape. True knowledge knows no uniformity. All leaps in knowledge occur *sideways*: the way knights move on chessboards.

Anything that grows in a straight line and in a predictable manner is without significance. It is the skewed and particularly the lateral knowledge that is decisive.

Aphorisms may not offer Truth, but they do offer the diverse, skewed, surprising truths I delight in answering to.

• • •

The world is a strange mixture of mystery and circularity.

Thoughts are like nights: the clear ones are always beautiful and cold.

The modern search for truth too often seems like a search for some loophole.

Where to turn? The whole guidebook is dog-eared.

We believe in the authentic mostly because we think we see it in other people.

According to Joseph Campbell, the main lesson of the myths through the ages and across cultures is that one might actually, deep within, be sovereign, that one's true self is majestic. Does anyone believe this anymore? Now, if you want people to go on quests, to change their lives, it might be better to tell them, *You were not born to reign, but neither were* they...

If only I had wished for a young man's life of mistakes and repentances, long stretches of shame illuminated by moments of inspiration, then I would have everything I wanted.

Eros is eros is eros.

For every spasm, an ism.

Going to the wound as if it were a nipple.

As the critic yawns, you can see his fangs.

Make It New! Make It Stick!

What a blessed time we live in! So many still want
their fifteen minutes of fame, though, soon, all will
crave just one moment of privacy.

Suffering warps what it fails to unlock.

The boy cried *Wolf!* so many times, the wolf finally came.

The sad promise of stars, which, because so far away,
at least seem close together –

The terrible ratio of petals to perfume!

Stephen Dobyns

An aphorism is a nondiscursive symbol of affective life. It's a right brain activity. That's where it is produced and that's where it is understood. This is also true of metaphor and art in general. What may be said discursively – "The poor resent charity." – may be said nondiscursively: "The hissing starts in the free seats." The latter comes from W.S. Merwin's wonderful *Asian Figures*, a collection of aphorisms and aphoristic narrations that I've been reading happily for forty years.

It pleases me that each side of the brain has its own way of speaking: discursively and nondiscursively. It makes my life seem less confining. And I like that an aphorism or metaphor or symbol has a sense of immediacy. Their meanings strike us all at once; and then, as we ponder them, they tell us more. "Nothing that is complete breathes," writes Antonio Porchia, again in Merwin's translation. I can brood about that for a long time. Its beauty strikes me, and I imagine I learn something about being human.

At first, I think, I was drawn to riddles, which led me to the Anglo Saxon riddles of the *Exeter Book*, which are also poems. A riddle is often an image and we're asked to guess the context. In second grade, I was asked, "Why did the moron throw his pants out the window?" Answer: "Because a boy outside was shouting, 'Free Press!'"

But here is a riddle from the *Exeter Book.* The answer is *Ice.*

I saw the night   going on its way.

It was splendidly,   wonderfully arrayed.

The wonder was on the wave: water become bone.

Then, in my book of poems *Griffon*, I published several dozen of my own riddles, though I cheated by putting the answer first.

My favorite is "Silence."

I am the music you were born to.
Then you put me aside, wanting your own;
like sticks scratching together, you wanted your own.
I am the song you will sing longest.

I am the clothing you were born in.
Then you changed me for bright reds and blues;
like a clown or bridegroom you wanted everything perfect.

Death is a marriage; you will wear me to the wedding.
I am the house you were born in.
Then you left me and went traveling;
Like a child without parents or fortune you went traveling.
I am where you are going.

"Silence" isn't an aphorism, but it is aphoristic and I can make aphorisms from it, such as: "Silence is the music we were born to."

Aphorisms aren't poems, but they are built of the same material. So, as a poet, I am drawn to write them. One difficulty with being a writer is that language is always a diminishment of idea. No matter how successful I think one of my poems, I have to admit that it remains incomplete. And so I keep writing, trying to approach my basic subjects from different directions. Writing aphorisms, for me, is an attempt to discover new approaches.

• • •

When you tell me something, I want you to be saying the words I hear, not the words you tell me.

Thief blames the open window.

Wolf's got a big smile – somebody's unhappy.

A box of cobwebs, the self he protected for so long.

Young, he thought the answers lay ahead; older now,
he thinks they must lie behind.

Even his tombstone was crooked.

Mouse grows proud, invites the cat to tea.

This one was kind because he had not yet been hurt.
That one was kind because he had been hurt often.

Your children's uncertainty when they look at you.
Isn't this a condemnation?

Once won a horse race, now he claims to tell the
future.

Crawls on his belly, calls it tact.

He never minded his faults until they blossomed in his children.

Tears his coat into ten pieces, calls it a wardrobe.

Love doesn't need a reason; hate needs a reason.

Scratches his balls when he thinks; scratches his head when he pees.

Resembles the dog on the brink of an idea.

When he worries, he imagines he thinks.

He calculates the cost of future sins in terms of past apologies.

Only when the phone rings past midnight does he remember what he owes the world.

He walked beside his false self as a child walks beside an older brother.

Sweet to its mate: the porcupine's kisses.

More prayers than the pope, but don't lend him money.

Gave a dime to a beggar, took it back when he wasn't thanked.

What frightened him was that there might be no mystery – only cash registers, politicians and the horizon.

Dangerous: your boss suggests you shut the door.

Dawdle: endeavor's disavowal.

Daydreamer: ambition minus action.

Ideologue: robot with a smile.

Ineffable: qualities lacking clear monetary value.

Inexhaustible: your helpmate's list of helpful suggestions.

Lobotomy: On most people the scars don't show.

Melodramatic: he forgot her mother's birthday.

Memory: sawdust heaped outside a mill.

Menace: fifteen passing for eighteen.

Alfred Corn

Aphorisms: I'm not sure at what age I learned the term. But, quite early, I relied on proverbs like "A stitch in time saves nine" and "Faint heart ne'er won fair lady." I relied on proverbs mainly as guides to conduct, in trivial or crucial instances. Gradually, my sense of the genre expanded, and I understood that proverbs could also distill observations about human behavior like, "The squeaky wheel gets the oil." I did not take this to mean I should start squeaking, even if experiencing painful friction.

The "stitch that saves nine" and the "squeaky wheel" are metaphors of course, and at some point I began to appreciate these wise sayings as metaphoric inventions, quite apart from their instructive content. I came to see them as literary objects based on striking comparisons – for example, Chamfort's "Most authors of collections of poetry or witty sayings resemble people who have a plate of cherries or oysters, first choosing the best and then eventually eating all of them." An increased understanding of how irony and concision work in literary texts helped me receive the full impact of La Rochefoucauld's maxims, for example, this one: "We all have strength enough to bear the sufferings of other people." And finally an exposure to Eastern religions and Zen koans led me to see that the truth – philosophical or oracular—is often best expressed with a certain mystery. As, for example, when Antonio Porchia says, "Whoever speaks the truth says almost nothing at all." True. Yet we press on, trying to speak it instead of remaining silent. Sometimes the medium we use – stitch, rod, wheel, oyster – is the aphorism.

• • •

To put "fine writing" into personal letters is like setting off fireworks in daylight.

In the twentieth century all the arts aspired to the condition of music, with the frequent exception of music itself.

The first deterrent to pointing out another person's failings is the certainty that we will then have to hear a long, heated defense of them.

As much by their weaknesses as their strengths do artists come into their own.

On the "chessboard" of life, there are always a few who play the darting, hobbled, two-phased, errant role of the knight.

There is something of Don Quixote in Don Juan; and vice versa.

Abstract-expressionist paintings are like childless couples, self-referential instead of producing external images, and, for that reason, more vehement than families with children or representational paintings.

Any mirror gazed at too long becomes stagnant.

The first of anything is also a last, the last time it will be first.

We all have differing "takes" on mutual friends, and, after a friend dies, those differences become, in time, even more marked.

Who do we think we are, to have so little self-acceptance?

Can we appreciate fine art without also appreciating ourselves for belonging to the small circle of those who do?

The idea of justice is inseparable from gravity; which explains why Themis represented as holding a balance suspended in her right hand.

One virtue of opera to its fans is that, in discussing a particular performance, they may themselves rise to operatic heights of ecstasy or fury.

Life wounds everyone. Besides blood, though, the artist also sheds light.

Like nearly everyone else, snobs fear death, but in their case the fear is unconscious and takes the form of an anxious grasping at what seems secure, enviable, and permanent. Superior to most things in life, they will – who knows? – perhaps also be above dying.

Having been found "guilty" of poverty, they were soon found guilty of many other things that wouldn't have been laid to their charge had they been adequately funded.

Eventually we learn not to try to meet the *person* who wrote the book we admire extremely; and thus better understand the luster that death adds to authors of the classics.

It's human to hope one day to have the leisure money offers to place spiritual values higher than material.

Divorce often brings an honesty and directness, an intimacy, that was unavailable during marriage.

I care for those not yet born and am also able to see doing so as partly a form of self-flattery.

The senses, when glorified, turn into idle, bloated aristocrats. Reason, when deified, becomes a superstition. The imagination, when subpoenaed, vanishes into thin air.

Bread you have earned may not taste as sweet as the cake selectively allocated at the palace, but it is better for your digestion.

Mixed motives need not discredit each other. When one rich person marries someone equally rich, only a purist would object that economic objectives had been tainted by any actual love.

The fundamental anxiety in writing arises from the contradiction of being entirely oneself *for others* – an aesthetic instance of the dilemma faced by anyone who tries to be honest and social at the same time.

Although absolute monarchs regard themselves as above the law, they still obey etiquette.

People will, occasionally, forgive you for the wrong you have done to them, but never for the wrong they have done to you.

When, after several tries, we don't understand an author, the suspicion hardens that he didn't, either.

The fear that there is no life after death is a vaster analogue of the apprehension that we will have to sleep the night alone.

On our bookshelves are volumes we have reread (some, many times), others we have read once only, others we pretend to have read, others we will in fact one day read, and, finally, some whose pages we won't live long enough to turn.

One lesson aphorisms (and poems) teach is that the felt impression of truth is partly a *rhythmic* or even a musical sensation.

What is the point of being brilliant unless you can at the same time be intelligent?

Exactly to the degree that fireworks astonish, they are conversation-stoppers.

So much easier to be saintly in letters than face to face – which accounts for the higher percentage of writing dealing with goodness than the actual goodness found in human behavior.

Another vain hope, like the wish that nations would stop waging war or that people's words and deeds wouldn't have double meanings.

A moral guide even more persuasive than a "pillar" of longstanding virtue is the transgressor who only this week took stock and now cries out, "What have I done?"

Both shopkeepers and artists know that setting up a mirror is an effective tactic if you want to disarm anyone dropping in to have a look at the wares.

One of the chief earmarks of the coward is cruelty toward his subordinates.

Wisdom never grins but only smiles; nor does the smile erase every line that sadness has inscribed in her face.

With its oscillation between the categories of mutability and permanence, photography is the contemporary poet's Grecian Urn.

Laughter is the homage that reason pays to unreason.

This amalgam of memory and speculation about the future, perceived as a forward-rushing motion on an oiled track, this vanishing act, that we call the present.

We do not praise those we envy or envy those we praise – evidence that there is always some hypocrisy in our official positions on what we value.

Might not children be our greatest alibi? For timidity, for compromise, the childless have only themselves to blame.

I'm always touched watching how those in conversation with someone who speaks non-standard English themselves gradually fall into pidgin.

The beloved body, our own Judas, after so many years of devoted service, hands us over to death – yes, and sometimes with a preliminary kiss.

All choice is error; but in refusing to choose, we still do choose.

Modernity is based on the desire to be independent, to follow no law but the commandments of desire.

Of the two phenomena, marriage and pornography, pornography is the more modern.

Eric Nelson

I don't think of myself as an aphorist, and I'm quite sure that I couldn't write an aphorism on demand. I'm a poet, but I sometimes write very short poems that are aphoristic in the sense that they are more declarative than descriptive, more abstract than concrete. Why I'm inclined to write some of my poems this way is my mom's doing.

My mom was a repository of proverbs, maxims, folk sayings, quotable quotes. She seemed to have some catchy-sounding bit of wisdom for any occasion. She fired them off without attribution, so it took me a while to discover that her expressions weren't of her own making but came from a variety of sources, ranging from the Bible to Ben Franklin to Shakespeare to Oscar Wilde to who-knows-who. I still don't know the source of some of them. One of her often repeated sayings was "to you a swallow is a summer," which she said almost exclusively to my dad. I don't remember any specific context for this comment, nor did I understand what she was telling him (though I could tell it wasn't a compliment). Nevertheless, I loved the sound of that phrase and the authority of it, even though for a long time I thought "a swallow" referred to what you do with your throat, which made the statement all the more mysterious and fascinating.

To my sisters and me she said more than once – after we'd ignored her request to straighten our rooms or perform some other duty – "I've nurtured vipers to my bosom." She said it with such dramatic flourish, and I was so intrigued by the image and the deliciously sinister word "vipers," that I realized it was less a scolding than a performance.

My mom had a fairly cynical world view, which she conveyed to us with two of her most frequent gnomic utterances: "no good deed goes unpunished," and "if you feed the pigeons, expect to get crapped on." How could I not love the paradox of the former and the inescapably vivid imagery of the latter? I also remember her saying as a sort of all-purpose bit of wisdom: "at night all cats are gray," a statement that always mystified me, but again, I delighted in the picture it created in my mind.

When I went off to college, she presented me with a new, hefty edition of *Bartlett's Quotations*, telling me that it would come in handy. I rolled my eyes and acted deeply apathetic. But her affinity for pithy expressions and well-phrased insights had rubbed off on me, and secretly I was pleased to have that book. I spent many hours over the years browsing through it. It was where I discovered the sources of some of her expressions. Over thirty years later, I still have it – well worn, dog-eared, underlined and highlighted.

But it wasn't until I was a sophomore English major that I began to think of aphorisms as a serious and complex use of language. It was William Blake's "Proverbs of Hell" that first blew my mind. Blake's aphorisms were full of contradiction and ambiguity and insight. "The cut worm forgives the plow;" "the road of excess leads to the palace of wisdom;" "sooner murder an infant in its cradle than nurse unacted desires" – these were new and intriguing and exciting to me.

I began writing poetry seriously at about this time, and although I wasn't conscious of it, the impulse toward aphorism was already part of my sensibility. It was natural for me to include aphoristic phrasing in my poems. Like poetry, aphorisms are as much about language as they are about meaning. So to me it seemed fitting for my aphorisms to use line breaks the same way they are used in poetry – for emphasis, rhythm, surprise. I began to think of those aphoristic lines as highly compressed, self-contained poems, and I put them in a file I called "Smalls."

So even though I still think of my "Smalls" as poems, I'm honored to have them called aphorisms and to be included in this collection.

• • •

Only someone who still has it
Can say
Hope is a curse.

Happy memories
Are the saddest.

It's solitude if you like it.
Loneliness if you don't.

Beneath the heaviest stone
A worm can live.
But who wants to live
Like a worm?

History is written by the winners,
Literature by the losers.

God's humor:
Lightning, then thunder.
The attack, then the warning.

Godless, the wounded cat
Heals itself
With its own rough tongue.

The belled cat learns
To stalk more softly.

No matter how high the jet,
Its shadow remains
On the ground.

The dead know nothing,
The only thing
We can't imagine.

The rain finds paths
We didn't know
Were there.

Just because you don't feel pain
Doesn't mean
You haven't hurt yourself.

You never step in the same river twice.
But the same shit, yes.

Sooner do nothing
Than waste time.

Only the dead are good.

Better to hate yourself
Than others.

Whether we see them or not
There are always stars
Always falling.

James Geary

There is a saying among journalists – shorter is harder – that alludes to the fact that a 10-word caption is more difficult to write than a 1,000-word article, which, in turn, is more difficult to write than a 10,000-word article. The difficulty lies in the need to keep so much in while leaving so much out. A good caption is like a good aphorism: Both convey essence as well as information with verve and freshness, and without merely stating the obvious. For the writer, crafting a truly original aphoristic sentence is the ultimate formal challenge.

For the reader, aphorisms are inspiringly pessimistic. I've often wondered, sometimes worried, why my favorite sayings are so dark, like Cyril Connolly's "Life is a maze in which we take the wrong turning before we have learnt to walk." I think it's because the apparent pessimism of the form is really an inverted optimism. We typically don't need much convincing to look on the bright side, but the writer who sheds darkness on things does us a great service. Aphorisms are inoculations, shots in the arm that boost our existential immune systems and help us see better in the dark.

• • •

To see clearly, one must very often squint.

A smile looks a lot like a wince.

For the best view, look askance.

You can never look in the same mirror twice.

It's hard to think clearly in someone's arms.

Never trust an animal – no matter how many legs it has.

Young people should picnic in active volcanoes.

We begin and end in beds.

There are certain mistakes we enjoy so much that we are always willing to repeat them.

There is always time between beginnings to do the whole thing over again.

In the margin for error lies all our room for maneuver.

There is not much room for error in an eggshell.

Advice is given freely because so much of it is worthless.

You must understand a thing completely before you can safely ignore it.

To get your foot in the door, first get it out of your mouth.

An animal must feel at least temporarily safe in order to really enjoy a meal.

Preparing for something brings it about.

Life: Adjusting a necktie in a funhouse mirror.

A door slammed in your face: The sound of opportunity knocking.

Dare to be unprepared.

Never be serious in public.

Burn your ships at night and in the morning build
bridges.

A thread's only strength is clinging.

When in doubt, remain in doubt.

Too many facts spoil the plot.

The numinous is the nitty-gritty.

Not many people live in the desert.

Sometimes, two goldfish in a bowl are enough.

Thomas Farber

Dubious – or squeamish – about the enterprise, some people inquire, "What motivates your epigrams?" Well ... occasionally, they ensue from hearing a word or phrase as if for the first time, awakening to sound, to layered meaning. Revealing or explicating latent or forgotten life in language. Inevitably, written response entails shaping, compressing – the eros of craft.

Sometimes, however, the impulse is a hunger to get at what's going on in our behavior, a conviction there is something that must be understood. A "there is some shit we will not eat," kind of deal. Think of the word *cant:* an inauthentic expression of piety (from Latin, to chant, as in wheedling, importuning). When cant provokes dismay, epigram may emerge.

And let us not forget the paradoxical thrill of working so unmarketable a form. Think of how skateboarding used to be. Endless discipline, endless repetition, to achieve proficiency in a field lacking dollar value in a culture that is all about dollars.

Still, one would not want to live in a world of only epigrams. (Jonathan Swift: in the mirror of satire "Beholders do generally discover every body's face but their Own." Adorno: "When love can only express itself by hatred for the inappropriate, one may come to resemble what one hates." William Matthews: "From Martial I learned foremost how important is to find ways to be angry with human folly and failure and to be forgiving of it at the same time…").

Head on pillow, the epigrammist mutters his own phrase, *riddled with perfections*. He expects, when he wakes, to write it down.

• • •

Jealousy's geometry: no right triangles.

Less that he wanted a divorce, more that he wished for his wife a new husband.

Wife's pang before betraying her husband: pre-coital *tristesse*.

Wrong, to assume hypocrites are without regret.

"When we start to die," something he once thought began in old age.

200

"Had they only been loved," something he once thought referred to the unhappy exception.

Given that he was honest at heart, his hypocrisy was pure pretense.

"I just don't understand you," said the man who believed he understood himself.

Misanthropy: overexposure.

'Source amnesia,' as, when you offer a sexual surprise to your lover, she asks, "Where did you learn that?"

The future. That which we can't yet remember.

Suicide. By gun – ninety percent success rate; by jumping from heights – thirty-three percent. Choose one.

Occupational hazards. Of marriage: rage – anger at the one to whom you are closest. Of being single: depression – anger at the one to whom you are closest.

So intuitive, the old, certain something bad will happen soon.

Older man, putting on quite a bit of weight. Fattening himself for the slaughter.

Not comfortable sharing; low need for affiliation. An only child, he became an only adult.

Kevin Griffith

I was on a radio talk show reviewing books recently and happened to read on the air a one-sentence short story by Lydia Davis, entitled "Bloomington." The story was aphoristic, of course, and being an aphorism aficionado, I thought everyone would share my enthusiasm for the short and pithy. I was wrong. My colleagues on the show skewered the story, blurting out reactions like "I hope she's not being paid by the word," and "how can you call that a story? You can't get lost in it!" When I told them how I loved how it read like an aphorism, their response was "what is that?"

I first became enamored of aphorisms after reading *Meditations* by Marcus Aurelius. The stoicism of Aurelius marked a man so world-weary as to be impervious to any of life's annoyances. Aurelius was the emperor of "staying centered," to use the parlance of self-help manuals. Yet he was also very funny. Or at least I thought so. Anytime I was caught up in the weltschmerz of the writing life – worried about where my next publication would come from, plagued with jealousy that some colleague had landed something in Tin House – there was Aurelius: "People out for posthumous fame forget that the Generations To Come will be the same annoying people they know now"

(Book Eight, 44). That's right, the descendants of the same darn people who are ignoring my genius now will be ignoring it in the future. You can't win. So, Aurelius says, "Uncomplicate yourself" (Book Four, 26).

My introduction to aphorisms through Marcus Aurelius led me to Nietzsche, Wittgenstein, James Richardson's *Interglacial*, and even George Carlin's *Brain Droppings*. As most aphorisms are indeed one-liners, they forced me to see my poetry in a new way too. At about the same time I was discovering the aphorism, I was struggling through a poetry manuscript, slogging through the usual submission/rejection cycle of the manuscript competition racket.

Aphorisms gave me a new insight. I should uncomplicate not only myself, but also my poetry. I began to see that most everyone's poems (with the possible exception of Yeats' – but hey, who can top him anyway?) could basically be pared down to one good line. Throwing caution to the wind, that is just what I did to my manuscript. Instead of a scalpel, I used a chainsaw on each of them, reducing them to their one-line essence. And it was good! I had so much fun I began writing nothing but one-line poems for a while, catching them as they poured out of my mind, and called the manuscript *My Book of Poetry*. And the first competition I sent it to selected it as a finalist. Thus, my loyalty to the form was secured.

• • •

Sartre said, "Hell is other people." But I just know deep inside that he wasn't talking about me.

Have you ever noticed how the Virgin Mary's face looks like a potato chip?

Things fall apart. The center cannot hold. So what else is new?

If only I could find the word that describes the feeling you get when you can't find the right word.

Live each day as if it were your last. And so I did. But it was a terrifying day, as I kept realizing that I was only a few hours away from death.

It is impossible for each person to be the bigger person.

If Hitler survived, he would still be dead by now.

Every word is a lazy anagram of itself.

An empty bookshelf still holds its own weight.

Hope is the tree house you have been building in your basement.

Freedom isn't free. But you do get a large drink with every purchase.

I would live forever if it didn't have to be with me.

The tree in the forest fell on my recording equipment.

You are the problem you fear most.

If death is the mother of beauty, then who is the mother-in-law?

A sad house opens its windows to let the dark out.

The enemy of my enemy is sometimes the best I can do when dating.

With God all things are possible. So how about a good health plan?

Aphorisms: Literature that has uncomplicated itself.

Silence: a chorus of mimes.

Sometimes life is like that guy who brings a book of dirty jokes to a baby shower. The gift is completely unacceptable, and why in the heck was he there in the first place?

Mom spelled backwards is Mom. And Dad is Dad. There is no escape.

Teamwork: There *is* a "u" and "i" in "quit."

Sun-ripened tomatoes: Yes. Sun-ripened chicken: No.

What can I say about aphorisms that hasn't already been said in an aphorism?

Why embrace death when one can write more aphorisms?

If a novel is a marriage, and a poem is a one-night stand, an aphorism is the knowing wink across a crowded room.

You can never have too many or two few aphorisms.

The only good aphorism is still a good aphorism.

A world without aphorisms would still contain this one.

An aphorism is the well-trained acrobat in the flea circus of the soul.

The opposite of an aphorism is another aphorism.

Between no more and no less is the aphorism.

All aphorisms great and small are great and small.

John Bradley

I can still remember stumbling on a copy of Antonio Porchia's *Voices,* translated by W. S. Merwin, in a used bookstore in Minneapolis in the early 1970s, my first encounter with the aphorism. The cover – a Magritte print of a man with wings on a bridge, his back to a sitting lion – was as enigmatic as the work inside. I had never heard of Porchia, and I didn't know what to make of his writing, which at the time I would have called *sayings*. Unlike the sayings I heard from my mother. But Porchia's sayings appealed to me. I liked their distilled nature. And I liked their mysteriousness. Yet they weren't poetry. At least not how I expected a poem to appear, with line breaks and stanzas. Porchia's aphorisms seemed like outcasts from a philosophy book, or maybe feral sayings from an apocryphal book of the Bible.

And yet the aphorism *is* poetic, resembling a fragment of a Sappho poem. It could be a cousin of Chinese fortunes or Japanese haiku, or even the paltry pun, but it's much easier to say what an aphorism is not.

It's not a t-shirt saying, and certainly not a bumper sticker slogan. It's not a marketing mantra, nor a riddle, nor zen koan. It's not the punch line of a joke you've missed, and it's definitely not something you'd find on a grave stone, though I wouldn't be surprised if someone hasn't tattooed one on his or her flesh.

I once saw in a textbook a list of aphorisms to be used as writing prompts for composition students. One of the aphorisms has stuck with me for over thirty years. They do that, clinging to stray corners of the brain. This one sure did:

Money is the best deodorant.

–ELIZABETH TAYLOR

As memorable as it is, my creative memory had slightly altered this to "Celebrity is the best deodorant." Time has proven Taylor's original aphorism much truer than my misremembered version.

My own path to the aphorism came long after using them as writing prompts. I had been writing prose poems for quite a while and began to wonder – how small can a prose poem be and still be a prose poem? Can it still breathe and have a pulse if only a line or two? Well, yes and no. After much experimenting, I realized that the one or two line prose poem often took on another personality. I was starting to write aphorisms.

Voices was the only book Antonio Porchia wrote in his lifetime. I suspect it was his *Leaves of Grass*, a book that slowly grew over many years as he fed and watered and nurtured his aphorisms.

Porchia must have the last word: "They will say that you are on the wrong road, if it is your own."

• • •

She lets me speak to her elbow, but not her clavicle.

Sometimes my thumb is bigger than the moon. That's when I know I'm smaller than my own thumb.

Unkempt sparrow song will thrive long after the last library crumbles.

Handwriting, no matter how shaggy or crude, grows in beauty the longer the creator's absence.

He tunneled his way out of Sing Sing only to emerge, years later, wiping dirt from his eye in a cell in Gitmo.

All the music in a river. All the silence in an ice cube.

Smoke needs no passport.

Rain speaks many dialects, yet no one ever requires a translator.

Never dine on someone else's shadow.

Sign post over the exit of the labyrinth: *Let us know if we can do anything to make your journey more difficult.*

The hole is sometimes greater than the sum of its parts.

Say, I left a bear trap in the kitchen to catch that confounding fly.

Whoever invented the pocket attempted to make up for the body's one great deficiency.

On the last morning he lived, Mussolini took a pee.

When Very Little Is Required in the Classroom: On Teaching the Long-Winded Writer to Write Short

BY SARA LEVINE

I am a big fan of littleness: essays the size of handkerchiefs, novels the length of nosebleeds, philosophies reduced to paragraphs. Years ago, when I was a graduate student, I was assigned to teach an upper-level group of undergraduates how to write arguments. There couldn't have been a worse match, the twenty-five-page essay and me. I drew Stephen Toulmin's six-part diagram for good arguments on the blackboard; I assigned long, complex discourses and broke them down, like cardboard boxes, into *claims*, *warrants*, *backings*; I spoke fervently about logical operators and qualifiers; and then, as soon as I was free to choose my *own* classes, I began to teach the aphorism.

The aphorism: conclusion detached from tedious argument. The aphorist says: "I am going to make a claim in one sentence, and make it so neatly and squarely, the reader will be dazzled and convinced – or unconvinced, but tough noogies, *she'll* have to figure out what led me to this."

These days I teach in a graduate level creative writing program, where many students have ambitions to write The Great American Novel. They are ready to pour out large quantities of writing about their lives, or their feelings, or their feelings about other people's lives. I never tell them not to do this, but certainly by asking them to consider the aphorism, I slow them down. I say, "Let's survey the range of prose genres and start with the shortest one. We'll do a sentence, one sentence at a time. Then you can work your way up to those things you want to write, those... paragraphs, those pages, those doorstops, I mean, novels."

At first this looks easy. Here is something manageable. The student is asked to write only one sentence. Then it becomes plain that to write a sentence is not enough. A sentence consists of a noun and a verb (Jane kicks) but an aphorism must have a pattern – a turn – or it doesn't sound like an aphorism at all.

I ask each student to write an aphorism on an index card and pass the index card to the person on his left; we tweak, we tinker, we try to improve. A skeptical student objects: *Can* one write an aphorism by *committee*? "You inhabit another character's imagination when you write a novel," I answer. "So write an aphorism for a character who isn't you." But it always proves harder than it sounds. When the work is done, we spread the index cards out on a table and discover they resemble, not a page from *Geary's Guide to the World's Great Aphorists*, but a row of hospital beds. Sentence after ailing sentence: punctured paradoxes, sprained metaphors, hobbled clauses, a ward of amputees!

These first lessons in writing aphorisms are lessons in failure. But I love failure as much as I love the aphorism. Not because I'm a masochist, but because each time your aphorism lands with a thud, you come closer to understanding the form. The feelings of inferiority or humility that come along with the experience of writing a truly lousy aphorism are fiddlesticks compared to a sharper understanding of how Dorothy Parker packs a big idea into a carry-on bag.

Style and Syntax

The aphorism is, in essence, a crash course in prose style.

For example, because it favors certain grammatical forms, the aphorism is a superb way to begin a conversation about syntax. The most frequently discussed aphoristic form is, of course, the chiasmus – the ABBA pattern by which two terms get crisscrossed. Reading a good chiasmus is like watching a resourceful cook make a satisfying meal out of two ingredients from the furry back of your refrigerator.

Knut Rockne:

When the going gets tough, the tough get going.

Karl Kraus:

Journalists write because they have nothing to say, and have something to say because they write.

Samuel Johnson to an aspiring writer:

Your manuscript is both good and original; the part that is good is not original, and the part that is original is not good.

Of course, not every aphorism is a chiasmus, but students quickly discover that in the aphorism, certain arrangements of clauses won't fly. The aphorism favors symmetry. Asyndeton. Parataxis. Abrupt movement. It also favors a nominal as opposed to verbal style, by which I mean that the verbs tend to fade into the background. This is a curious difference from other forms of prose writing. When teaching practitioners of the essay, the prose poem, the short story, and the novel, I squeeze a bellows over that ashy heap of Student Vocabulary, trying to discover how the right verb might flare up and ignite the whole sentence, but eh, not so much in the aphorism. Here we like the dull verbs that lend themselves to existential statement.

Robert Louis Stevenson:

To travel hopefully is a better thing than to arrive.

Or this from Wallace Stevens:

Poetry is a pheasant disappearing in the brush.

Disappear! Aah, *there's* a dynamic verb, you can hear the rustle of its feathers, but it's been relegated to the subordinate clause. Likewise in Stevenson, where the verbs "to travel" and "to arrive" occupy the nominal slots

in the sentence, the main verb is that wan but useful "is,"
useful since the aphoristic impulse is to define, to cut
off, to say this is how something is, for all time, now and
evermore.

Balance the Concrete with the Abstract

Apprentice writers are often urged to be specific,
concrete, and sensory, and above all, to "write what
they know!" But the best writers move nimbly back and
forth between stylistic poles (specific, general; abstract,
concrete; figurative, literal); the best writers can describe
the present moment but also get outside of its sticky net;
which is why I fret a little when we narrow the literary arts
to what you can see, feel, taste, touch, and smell.

Luckily, the aphorism provides a marvelous corrective.
The aphorist may say "I." The aphorist may write in
the present tense (to suggest her perpetual claim to
truth). But the aphorism is not interested in language
that "reproduces" experience so much as language that
purports to master it. It does not fear abstraction, though
often what snags our attention is the way an aphorism pairs
abstraction with some arresting concrete image.

Leonard Cohen:

There is a crack in everything. It's how the light gets in.

Henri Michaux:

Consider precedents. They've tarnished everything
they've grasped.

By Week Two, I have instructed my students to go

home and write no more than *one* page of aphorisms on a chosen theme. When we meet again, they drop the page on my desk as if it were a used tissue – apologetically and with disgust. "When are we going to write in longer form?" a student asks, desperate to get out of the sentence and run free in the prairie of a paragraph – oh yes, a paragraph never looked so good! Those light and airy rectangles, those sweet little cakes of text! "Next week, micro-epic," I say and then insist we read their aphorisms aloud. The tweaking begins again. I arrange and re-arrange the words in their sentences with the concentration of a child rearranging dollhouse furniture. We talk about changes in sequence or diction. We talk about paradox and how it works in a line by Adolfo Bioy Casares:

How pleasant life would be if it ended a little before death.

How pleasant this class would be if it ended a little before three.

writes a student on the board. I say, "Good try, Bill. Aphorisms often work by subtle substitutions, but that doesn't work *at all* as an aphorism! Let's talk about why!"

And we do.

Tone

But in the end, we always talk about *tone.* For once we have covered the stylistic aspects, the students realize – or perhaps I browbeat them until they say they realize – that the aphorism is difficult to write because you have to sound sure of what you are saying. It is also difficult because the aphorist aims for a transgressive, or at least surprising, viewpoint. Sometimes a person triumphs over his doubts and achieves a rousing tone of conviction only to discover that what he is saying is as controversial as a piece of soap. We discuss the subtle, possibly gendered, differences between proverbs and aphorisms. Handed down orally from generation to generation, proverbs hardly seem to belong to their authors at all. *No use crying over spilled milk.* Who said that? More to the point, who hasn't?

Recently a student told me she liked aphorisms until I forced her to read so many at once, at which point it became a kind of Chinese water torture: one profound drip after another. I had assigned La Rochefoucauld's *Maxims*, I had assigned Lichtenberg's *Waste Book*. It is true, I think, that too many aphorisms taken at once – without food or drink or paragraphs – can cause the appetite to sicken. Too many at once can also induce skepticism about the genre's bad-ass stance. By "bad ass" – a technical term as useful as "chiasmus" – I mean the aphorist's tendency to revel, too often, in his own cynicism. There he is removing a mask, here he is pointing to a hypocrisy, there he is again, trying to ruin your marriage or your day.

Karol Bunsch:

The blossom withers, the thorn remains.

Leopardi:

One man's pleasure is another man's boredom.

La Rochefoucauld:

If we are to judge of love by its consequences,
it more nearly resembles hatred than friendship.

Madame de Stael:

The more I see of men, the more I love my dog.

Can you forgive a person for beginning to think
that aphorisms are all about the villainy of humankind,
the treachery of friends, the foolishness of lovers? Can
you forgive a teacher for worrying that she is stifling
her students who want to write about their spanking
fat happiness, their joy unencumbered by doubt and
cynicism, their appreciation of the exquisite in the
ordinary?

Then again, why should it matter if the aphorism is
dark and gloomy, when the aphorism is also so patently
provisional, unfinished, and partisan? These short
gnomic sayings don't offer extension, but they *provoke*
disagreement (claims, counter-claims, qualifications,
argument). Of course, the reader does the work *herself*.

It's a lazy form! E.M. Cioran said somewhere,
explaining why he chose it.

"Big book, big bore," said Callimachus – reminding us
that a master aphorist can even dispense with the verb.

Author Bios

Lily Akerman first began writing aphorisms in James Richardson's poetry class at Princeton, where she studied Comparative Literature, Theater, and Creative Writing. She moved to Dublin on a Fulbright and has been living there for the past year.

Charles Bernstein is author of *Recalculating* (University of Chicago Press, 2013), *Attack of the Difficult Poems: Essays and Inventions* (Chicago, 2011), and *All the Whiskey in Heaven: Selected Poems* (Farrar, Straus and Giroux, 2010). He is Donald T. Regan Professor of English and Comparative Literature at the University of Pennsylvania, where he is co-director of PennSound <writing.upenn.edu/pennsound>. More info at epc.buffalo.edu.

John Bradley grew up in Framingham, Massachusetts; Lincoln and Omaha, Nebraska; Massapequa and Lynbrook, New York; and Wayzata, Minnesota. He received his MA from Colorado State University and his MFA from Bowling Green State University. His book *Love-In-Idleness*, a collection of persona poems set in Fascist Italy, won the Washington Prize. More recent books include *Add Musk Here*, *Terrestrial Music*, and *War on Words*. He has received an Illinois Arts Council grant and a previous NEA Fellowship in Poetry. He has been teaching writing at Northern Illinois University since 1992. He lives in DeKalb, Illinois, with his wife, Jana, and cat, Luna.

Ashleigh Brilliant is the creator of *POT-SHOTS* and syndicated author of *I May not be Totally Perfect, but Parts of*

Me are Excellent. 10,000 copyrighted *Brilliant Thoughts* are available as cards, books etc. He is the world's highest-paid writer (per word).

Steven Carter is the author of fifteen books published in America and abroad, including six collections of aphorisms and the two-volume *The New Devil's Dictionary*. In 1989 he was awarded the Schachterle Prize by the National Society for Literature and Science. In 2000 he became the only two-time winner of Italy's coveted *Nuove Lettere* International Poetry and Literature Prize. A former Senior Fulbright Fellow at two Polish universities, he is Emeritus Professor of English in the California State University. Carter and his wife Janice divide the year between Arizona and Montana.

Some of his additional books are as follows: *Leopards in the Temple: Selected Essays 1990-2000*; *Bearing Across: Studies in Literature and Science*; *222: Aphorisms & Reflections (Volumes I-III)*; *Devotions to the Text*; *The Nothing That Is and The Nothing That Is Not: On Death, Dying, and Suffering*; *A Do-It-Yourself Dystopia: The Americanization of Big Brother*.

Christopher Cokinos is the author of *Hope Is the Thing with Feathers: A Personal Chronicle of Vanished Birds* and *The Fallen Sky: An Intimate History of Shooting Stars*, both from Tarcher/Penguin. The winner of a Whiting Award, Cokinos has traveled across the world, from Greenland to Antarctica, in search of the stories of science and history that inform his writing. Christopher Cokinos divides his time between Logan Canyon, Utah, and Tucson, Arizona, where he directs the creative-writing program at the University of Arizona and is affiliated faculty with the Institute of the Environment. His website is at www.christopher-cokinos.com.

Alfred Corn is the author of nine books of poems, the most recent titled *Contradictions*. Also, a collection of essays, *The Metamorphoses of Metaphor*, and a novel, *Part of His Story*. In 2008 the University of Michigan Press published *Atlas: Selected Essays, 1989-2007*. A new edition of *The Poem's Heartbeat*, his study of prosody, has just been brought out by Copper Canyon. Fellowships for his poetry include the Guggenheim, the NEA, an Award in Literature from the Academy of Arts and Letters, and one from the Academy of American Poets. He has taught at Yale, Columbia, and UCLA. He spends half of every year in London.

Stephen Dobyns' most recent book is a novel, *The Burn Palace*, published by Blue Rider/Penguin in February 2013. Palgrave released his second book of essays on poetry, *Next Word, Better Word,* in 2011. His most recent book of poems is *Winter's Journey* (Copper Canyon, 2010). His previous work of fiction is a book of short stories *Eating Naked* (Holt, 2000). His other work includes *Best Words, Best Order* (Palgrave, 2003), essays on poetry; *The Porcupine's Kisses* (Penguin, 2002), a book of prose poems, aphorisms and definitions, and *Velocities* (Penguin, 1994), a volume of new and selected poems. He has also published ten other books of poetry and twenty other novels. Two of his novels and two of his short stories were made into films. He has received a Guggenheim fellowship, three fellowships from the National Endowment of the Arts and numerous prizes for his poetry and fiction. Between 1995 and 2008, he published about thirty feature stories in the *San Diego Reader,* available at http://www.sandiegoreader.

com/staff/stephen-dobyns/. Dobyns teaches in the MFA Program of Warren Wilson College, and has taught at Sarah Lawrence College, Emerson College, Syracuse University, Boston University, University of Iowa and half a dozen other colleges and universities. He was born in New Jersey in 1941. He lives in Westerly, RI.

Sharon Dolin is the author of five poetry books, most recently: *Whirlwind* and *Burn and Dodge*, winner of the AWP Donald Hall Prize in Poetry. She has been awarded the 2013 Witter Bynner Fellowship from the Library of Congress, selected by Poet Laureate Natasha Trethewey. She lives in New York City where she teaches at the Unterberg Poetry Center of the 92nd Street Y and Poets House, directs The Center for Book Arts Annual Letterpress Poetry Chapbook Competition, and directs the Writing About Art in Barcelona poetry workshop. She also teaches Creative Writing at Rutgers University. Her aphorism sequences have been published in *Hotel Amerika*, *Seneca Review*, *Fourth Genre*, *American Poet*, *The Kenyon Review Online*, and *Denver Quarterly*. www.sharondolin.com

Olivia Dresher is a publisher, editor, anthologist, and writer of poetic fragments & aphorisms. Her poetry, fragments, and essays have appeared in anthologies and in a variety of on-line and in-print literary magazines. She is the editor of *In Pieces: An Anthology of Fragmentary Writing* and co-editor of the anthology *Darkness and Light: Private Writing as Art.* She has spontaneously written thousands of fragments & aphorisms at Twitter.com, where she has a large following, and plans to choose some of these for several in-print collections. Her complete bio and select writings can be found at OliviaDresher.com.

Thomas Farber is the recipient of Guggenheim, National Endowment, Rockefeller, Fulbright, and Dorothea Lange-Paul Taylor fellowships, author of many works of fiction, creative nonfiction, and the epigrammatic (including *Truth Be Told: New & Collected Premortems*, and *The Twoness of Oneness*). He is Senior Lecturer in English at the University of California, Berkeley. Visit www.thomasfarber.org

James Geary (www.jamesgeary.com) is the Deputy Curator of the Nieman Foundation for Journalism at Harvard University. He is the author of two books about aphorisms, *The New York Times* bestseller *The World in A Phrase: A Brief History of the Aphorism* and *Geary's Guide to The World's Great Aphorists*. His most recent book is *I Is an Other: The Secret Life of Metaphor and How It Shapes The Way We See The World*. He has performed his Juggling Aphorisms and Mixing Metaphors show – a lively mix of memoir, literary history, audience participation and live juggling of words and balls – throughout the U.S. and Europe.

Kevin Griffith, who teaches at Capital University, in Columbus, OH, is the author of many books, including a collection of prose poetry, *Denmark, Kangaroo, Orange* (2008), and a collection of micro-fiction, *101 Kinds of Irony* (2012). He has been awarded three Ohio Art Council Fellowships for Excellence in Poetry, the most recent being in 2014. He and his eleven-year-old son Sebastian recently released the website Brickjest.com, which recreates David Foster Wallace's 1,079-page novel *Infinite Jest* entirely in Legos.

James Guida grew up in Australia and currently lives in New York. He is the author of *Marbles* (Turtle Point Press, 2009) and contributes essays to *The New Yorker* online and other publications.

H. L. Hix teaches at the University of Wyoming. His recent poetry books include *Chromatic*, a finalist for the 2006 National Book Award, *God Bless*, a "political/poetic discourse" built around sonnets and sestinas and villanelles composed of quotations from George W. Bush, and *Legible Heavens*, which *Publishers Weekly* called "strange and fierce." In addition, he has collaborated on translations of Estonian and Lithuanian poetry, and written books of criticism including *As Easy As Lying: Essays on Poetry* and *Spirits Hovering Over the Ashes: Legacies of Postmodern Theory*.

Irena Karafilly was born in the Urals but has crossed several borders while learning to walk, talk, read, and write. She has lived in five countries, most recently in Greece, where the plot of *The Captive Sun* is set. She speaks several foreign languages badly, swears perfectly in Polish and Greek, and writes in English about beleaguered Greek villagers. She has been largely educated in Canada, the most generous of countries, where the lack of a high-school diploma proved to be no impediment to obtaining three university degrees. While still an undergraduate, Karafilly sold a short story to Bob Weaver at the CBC and has ever since been trying to write a bestseller so she could devote herself full time to her writing. She has worked as a secretary, administrator, editor, businesswoman, journalist, university lecturer, and writer, publishing dozens of poems and stories, while trying to survive as a single mother. Though fame and fortune remain elusive, her work has won several literary prizes, including the National Magazine Award and the CBC Literary Award. Her short stories have been broadcast, anthologized, and published in both commercial and literary magazines, in Canada and abroad. Author of five books, Karafilly has also written book reviews and travel articles, which have appeared in numerous newspapers, including the *New York Times* and the *International Herald Tribune*. She currently divides her time between Greece and Canada, still looking for Home.

Richard Kostelanetz

NNDB.com
Britannica.com
Who's Who in Hell
Postmodern Fiction
Contemporary Poets
Who's Who in America
Contemporary Novelists
Who's Who in the World
Who's Who in American Art
Directory of American Scholars
Advocates for Self-Government
Readers Guide to Twentieth-Century Writers
Baker's Biographical Dictionary of Musicians
Who's Who in U.S. Writers, Editors, and Poets
The Merriam-Webster Encyclopedia of Literature
The Facts on File Companion to American Poetry
The Facts on File Companion to 20th Century Poetry
Contemporary Jewish-American Dramatists and Poets
The Chronology of Webster's Dictionary of American Writers
The HarperCollins Reader's Encyclopedia of American Literature
The Greenwood Encyclopedia of Multiethnic American Literature
The Greenwood Encyclopedia of American Poets and Poetry

Yahia Lababidi is the author of *Signposts to Elsewhere*, a new book of aphorisms selected for "Books of the Year, 2008" by *The Independent*, UK. *Signposts*, is published by Jane Street Press – www.janestreet.org/press – and is currently being translated into Arabic (and, quite possibly Italian very soon). Lababidi's poems and essays have appeared in journals such as *Agni*, *Cimarron Review* and *Rain Taxi* as well as throughout Europe and the Middle East.

Ann Lauinger has written two books of poetry: *Persuasions of Fall* (University of Utah Press, 2004), winner of the Agha Shahid Ali Prize in Poetry, and *Against Butterflies* (Little Red Tree Publishing, 2013). Her work has appeared in publications from *Alimentum* to *Zone 3*, including *Common Ground Review, Hotel Amerika*, *Measure*, *Parnassus*, *The Same, Smartish Pace*, and *The Southern Poetry Review*. Poems have been anthologized in *Decomposition*, *The Bedford Introduction to Literature*, *Poetry Daily Essentials, 2007*, and *In a Fine Frenzy: Poets Respond to Shakespeare*; and have been featured on Poetry Daily, Verse Daily, and Martha Stewart Living Radio. A member of the literature faculty at Sarah Lawrence College and of the Slapering Hol Press Advisory Committee, she lives in Ossining, NY.

Sara Levine teaches Short Prose Forms and other MFA Writing courses at The School of the Art Institute of Chicago. Her work has appeared in *Conjunctions*, *Nerve*, *The Iowa Review*, *Caketrain*, and other magazines. She has won a Special Mention for Nonfiction in *The Pushcart Anthology*, three citations in *The Best American Essays*, and been anthologized in *The Touchstone Anthology of Contemporary Creative Nonfiction* and the forthcoming *Best of Fence*. She has a Ph.D. from Brown University and is a recipient of the Andrew W. Mellon Fellowship in the Humanities.

Dan Liebert is a worldwide traveler (over 42 countries)

and has lived in Amsterdam, Cairo, New York for many years, Santa Fe, and he now resides in a tiny town on the Ohio River in extreme southern Illinois. His aphorisms and one line poems have been published in *Yale Review*, *The London Review*, *Barrow Street*, *Michigan Quarterly Review*, *Sentence: A Journal of Prose Poetics*, and *Berkeley Poetry Review*. His translations of the poet Rumi, (*Rumi: Fragments, Ecstasies* by Omega Press) was the first truly modern Western translation of his work and has remained in print for 26 years. Along with writing classic aphorisms, he is the only writer in English of the one-line poetic-aphoristic "greguerias'" of Ramon Gomez de la Serna. He has won the Illinois Art Council $7,000 fellowship in poetry.

James Lough's book *This Ain't No Holiday Inn: Down and Out in New York's Chelsea Hotel 1980-1995* was published by Schaffner Press. His collection of nature essays, *Sites of Insight* won the Colorado Endowment for the Humanities Publications Prize, and *Spheres of Awareness: A Wilberian Integral Approach to Literature, Philosophy, Psychology, and Art* is a collection of philosophical essays. He has published over 80 articles, essays, and short stories, and served as an editor with *ArtPULSE* magazine, *The Denver Quarterly, Divide, Bastard Review, Document,* and *Artemis*. He is a professor of nonfiction writing for the Savannah College of Art and Design's writing department, which he formerly directed.

George Murray is a Canadian poet. He was the editor of the literary blog Bookninja.com, a contributing editor at *Maisonneuve* magazine, and a contributing editor at several literary magazines and journals. After several years abroad in rural Italy and New York City, in 2005 he returned to Canada. He now lives in St. John's, Newfoundland and Labrador. Murray's 2007 book, *The Rush to Here*, a sequence of 57 sonnets, reworks a number of traditional forms such as Petrarchan, Spenserian, and Shakesperian sonnets. His book, *Whiteout*, was published in April, 2012.

Eric Nelson directed the Department of Writing and Linguistics' creative writing program at Georgia Southern University, where he taught since 1989. His publications include four collections of poetry, including *Terrestrials* (2004), which was chosen by Maxine Kumin as the winner of the X.J. Kennedy Poetry Award, and *The Interpretation of Waking Life*, winner of the Arkansas Poetry Award (1991). His poems have appeared or are forthcoming in numerous journals and anthologies, including *Poetry*, *The Christian Science Monitor*, *The Southern Review*, *The Missouri Review*, *Oxford American*, *The Sun*, *The Best of the Bellevue Literary Review*, *Strongly Spent: Fifty Years of Poetry from Shenandoah*, and *A New Geography of Poets*. In 2005, he was named the Georgia Author of the Year in Poetry by the Georgia Writers' Association.

Hart Pomerantz is a Canadian lawyer and television personality, best known for his collaboration with *Saturday Night Live* producer Lorne Michaels in *The Hart and Lorne Terrific Hour*. However, Pomerantz is also well known to Canadian audiences through his many appearances as a regular on *This Is the Law*, where he brought a unique sense of irreverent humour to the show along with his legal knowledge. More recently, he was the host of the shortlived Prime series *Grumps*. He is a graduate of the University of Toronto Law School and currently resides in Toronto, Ontario.

James Richardson's *Interglacial: New and Selected Poems and Aphorisms* was a finalist for the 2004 National Book Critics Circle Award. His previous books include *Vectors: Aphorisms and Ten-Second Essays*, *How Things Are*, *As If*, *Second Guesses*, *Reservations* and two critical studies, *Thomas Hardy: The Poetry of Necessity* and *Vanishing Lives*. Winner of an Award in Literature from the American Academy of Arts and Letters, Richardson has recent work in Best *American Poetry 2001*, 2005 and 2009, *The New Yorker*, *Slate*, *Paris Review*, *Poetry Daily*, *Science News*, *American Religious Poems*, *Geary's Guide to the World's Great Aphorists*, and *Great American Prose Poems*. *Jääkausien väliltä*, a Finnish edition of 400 of his aphorisms, will appear this spring. He is Professor of English and Creative Writing at Princeton University.

David Shields is the author of ten books of fiction and nonfiction, including the *New York Times* bestseller *The Thing About Life is that One Day You'll be Dead* (which was published by Knopf and is now available as a Vintage paperback), *Reality Hunger: A Manifesto, Black Planet: Facing Race during an NBA Season* (a finalist for the National Book Critics Circle Award), *Remote: Reflections of Life in the Shadow of Celebrity* (winner of the PEN Revson Award), and *Dead Languages: A Novel* (winner of the PEN Syndicated Fiction Award). His work has been translated into German, French, Dutch, Norwegian, Portuguese, Turkish, Farsi, Korean, Japanese, and Chinese. The Chair of the 2007 National Book Awards nonfiction panel, he has received a Guggenheim fellowship, two NEA fellowships, an Ingram Merrill Foundation Award, a Ludwig Vogelstein Foundation grant, and a New York Foundation for the Arts Fellowship. His essays and stories have appeared in the *New York Times Magazine*, *Harper's*, *Esquire*, *Yale Review*, *Village Voice*, *Salon*, *Slate*, *McSweeney's*, and *Believer*.

Charles Simic is a Serbian-American poet and co-Poetry Editor of the Paris Review. In 2007, he was appointed the fifteenth Poet Laureate Consultant in Poetry to the Library of Congress. He has published twenty-eight books, and his

The World Doesn't End book of prose poems won the 1990 Pulitzer Prize. He has also won a MacArthur Fellowship in 1984, the Wallace Stevens award in 2007, and the Griffin Poetry Prize in 2004.

Alex Stein is the author of *Weird Emptiness*, a collection of aphorisms, mainly about poetry and poetics, of which the poet David Mason wrote: "Bracing, chastening, and furiously intelligent." Stein is also the author of *The Artist as Mystic: Conversations with Yahia Lababidi,* a collection of interviews on the subject of "transformation" in the aphoristic and journal-based writings of Kafka, Baudelaire, Nietzsche, Rilke, Kierkegaard and others. Stein is also the author of a collection of interviews and essays on subjects more social and political, *Made Up Interviews With Imaginary Artists*, (Ugly Duckling Presse) parts of which have been performed on stages in Colorado, New York, and San Francisco. He lives in Boulder, Colorado and works at the University of Colorado at Boulder.

Michael Theune is a poet and critic. He's published poems, essays, and reviews in numerous journals, including *The Iowa Review, The New Republic, Pleiades*, and *Verse*. He is the editor of *Structure & Surprise: Engaging Poetic Turns* (Teachers & Writers, 2007), the first book of poetry writing pedagogy to focus on the poetic turn as a significant element of poetic craft. He is an Associate Professor of English at Illinois Wesleyan University in Bloomington, Illinois.

Holly Woodward is a writer and artist. She combines her poems, calligraphy, painting and collage into handmade books. "Wanting," a small online chapbook, appears at Gold Wake Press. Four poems were published recently by Mezzo Cammin. Some prose is on the 92nd Y Unterberg poetry site, Podium. A sonnet is in the recent *Lavender Re-*

view. No one listens to me, especially on Twitter. If I want to make sure that nobody reads a work, I post in on my blog, "Wit's End." In the Urals, two friends drank at a bar and argued whether prose or poetry was nobler. The poet shot the prose writer. I write stories and poems, so I kill myself.